MADE EASY

Nutritious Organic Produce from Your Own Garden: A Step-by-Step Guide

by C. Forrest McDowell, PhD
& Tricia Clark-McDowell

Published by **Cortesia Press**
Cortesia Sanctuary
84540 McBeth Rd, Eugene, Oregon, USA, 97405

ISBN: 978-0-942064-73-5

Inquiries & Bulk Pricing:

1-866-837-5854 or info@onesanctuary.com
www.onesanctuary.com • www.homecompostingmadeeasy.com

Food Policy and the Need for Change

There is a growing "Earth-friendly" revolution taking hold — the desire to have more choice and control in the foods we consume. Food gardening at home, or in a community plot, is part of a broad shift in consciousness that focuses on wellness, nutrition and self-sufficiency. Personal or community food security allows households to provide more of their food needs and/or to share their harvest with others in need.

Home food gardening reacquaints us with optimally fresh, tasty and nutritious fruits and vegetables costing a fraction of store-bought produce that is often shipped long distances. It teaches children that fruits and vegetables come from the earth, not grown in grocery stores. It inspires us to be healthwise — to remember that *we are what we eat*. Importantly, food gardening can save us hundreds of dollars a year in food expenses.

If you want to save the Earth —
begin with the earth in your own backyard

The Old Model

Food policy today is primarily based on creating a dependent *consumer* whose needs are determined by government, large corporations, agribusinesses, politics, and media marketing. As a result, home food production and preservation in the U.S. has declined from 35% of households in 1870 to only 1% in 2005. Additionally (and in spite of scientific advances), people suffer from diminished health and healthcare, poor air, water and soil quality, and overprocessed, nutrient-poor foods.

Perhaps most detrimental to individuals is the loss of a heartfelt and informed connection to this Earth: its soil, water, air, habitat and species. Earth's natural resources are too often associated with commodities. As a result, people forget to live simply so that others, and this Earth, may simply live. They misplace the spirit of stewardship and generosity.

The New Model

The basic foundation of a new food policy restores informed choice as a *prosumer* — one who is empowered in their lifestyle habits and needs to be part of a broader solution to respect Earth's resources, to live within one's means, to commit to personal wellness, and to help others in need. It also brings the focus of food sufficiency to the local level — one's household, neighborhood and community. It supports local/regional family-based agriculture. Most importantly, a new food policy model restores personal confidence in knowing that we have a voice — personally, locally, nationally — in the well-being of our lives, the lives of others, and this Earth and all its resources and species.

This Book — One Small Step

It is our commitment — indeed, our hope — that this low-cost guide supports those initial steps to the jouney of a lifetime: not only to know the joy of co-creating with Nature, but to experience a new level of responsibility for your own health, nutritional, and food security needs. By caring for the Earth, may you be inspired to follow the way of the hummingbird: *To sip the nectar without bruising the flower.*

CONTENTS

Note: *To ensure optimal success, you may need to adapt techniques in this guide according to your region, growing zone, soil type & climatic conditions.*

How to Use This Guide

According to the Gardening Season — Follow the Steps for each season shown in the **Inside & Back covers**. Topic locations are shown in yellow sidebar

Gardening Basics — Information is organized by topic to easily guide you. You may find it helpful to progress from front to back in this booklet

Nutrition Connection & Charts — These topics are grouped in the middle pages of this guide, pp. 28-43

Welcome to Your Food Garden

This guide promotes an exciting new way of looking at gardening & nutrition: making conscious choices to garden so that Mother Earth is not harmed; and the vegetables & fruits you grow and harvest are ripe with nutritious value & taste for food safety and security.

Natural Gardening describes those respectful & Earth-friendly techniques (organic-based) used to enhance and maintain the overall health and productivity of the garden. We created **The Natural Garden Pyramid** and its *13 Guiding Principles* to provide both the practical and ethical foundation for your success. You will repeatedly find these 13 principles applied throughout this guide.

SAVE the PLANET

Plant a Seed of Hope
Respect the Earth
Harvest Your Good Efforts
~ Share ~

Benefits of Gardening

Quality Control
Optimal nutritious content of the food you eat

Saves Grocery $
$30-100+ monthly of fresh produce in only 100 sq ft

Bond with Nature
Creates lifelong skills for you and your family

Builds self-esteem
Food & exercise for the body, mind & spirit

Earth-friendly
Least harmful practices protect soil, beneficial wildlife, humans, pets

Community food security
allows households to meet more of their own food needs, potentially sharing their harvest with others in need

Our Gift to You

Our family has gardened the same plot of land for almost 25 years — our kids grew up barefoot in the strawberry patch! We began, however, by freely helping those in need in our community to grow food, herbs and flowers in raised-beds at their homes and shelters. Our nonprofit organization rallied dozens of volunteers and businesses to support our efforts.

Over the years we learned that a garden is a sanctuary — it deserves one's respect and stewardship of Nature. Soil is precious and must be reverently grown. Nutrient-rich soil preserves its microlife and helps create nutritiously rich vegetables and fruits.

Gardening, as a favorite leisure activity, is a huge industry that is supported by both its artistic and scientific endeavors and inquiries. Our commitment as professional gardeners, educators and writers, is to make gardening as easy to understand as possilbe. In our guides we strive to take out the "fluff" that fills so many gardening books. As certified Master Gardeners/Composters, we know the importance of accurate, concise information. May you do well in your gardening efforts. **May your garden give you joy and peace!**

Natural Garden Pyramid
A Guide to Gardening Choices

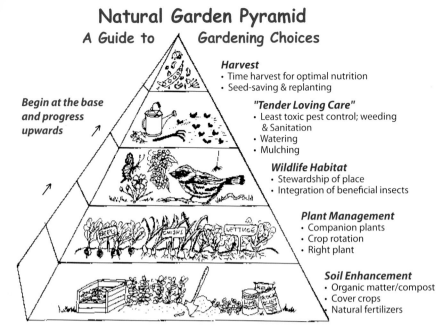

Begin at the base and progress upwards ↗ ↗

Harvest
- Time harvest for optimal nutrition
- Seed-saving & replanting

"Tender Loving Care"
- Least toxic pest control; weeding & Sanitation
- Watering
- Mulching

Wildlife Habitat
- Stewardship of place
- Integration of beneficial insects

Plant Management
- Companion plants
- Crop rotation
- Right plant

Soil Enhancement
- Organic matter/compost
- Cover crops
- Natural fertilizers

The **Natural Garden Pyramid** depicts a cyclical process initiated by good site selection and garden design. It seeks to nurture the soil, plants, beneficial insects and wildlife, and to maintain the overall health of the garden, from initial planting to harvest. In this way, natural gardening stewardship mimics nature by promoting diversity and balance, helping to co-create, regenerate and sustain the seasonal garden drama year-after-year. Part of the purpose of this guide is to give you basic information in using the 13 Principles shown in the figure above, as they progress upward from the pyramid's broad base. These principles of plant *and* soil health are briefly explained below, and in more detail in this guide.

13 Principles of Plant & Soil Health
(Based on the Natural Garden Pyramid)

1. Enhance soil quality & microlife through regular additions of organic matter, especially compost
2. Enrich soil through the planting of cover crops (green manures)
3. Use only natural fertilizers
4. Encourage plant health & diversity through companion planting (interplanting)
5. Practice crop rotation
6. Plant the right plant in the right place at the right time
7. Create habitat space that attracts certain wildlife (birds, frogs, critters, etc.)
8. Create vegetation habitat that attracts beneficial insects for pest control
9. Use least-toxic pest control; control weeds & practice good garden sanitation
10. Water deeply at the right time
11. Use mulches to conserve water & soil moisture, discourage weeds, and protect soil microlife
12. Time harvest for optimal nutrition
13. Use highest quality open-pollinated, non-GMO seeds/starts from your region (for durability) so that you can save seeds from plants for next year

Garden Design

Carefully planning the layout and design of your food garden, whatever its intended size, is essential for success. If you have a yard, patio, or deck, it is important to know where and how you will grow your produce. If your plot is part of a community garden, you should know about various factors that may affect production. Although there is much to consider, the following strategies & tips will certainly help you create a food garden that serves your needs.

Identify Features

On paper, draw or list important features in the yard or around your food garden:

Buildings
Shed, greenhouse
Fences & boundaries
Pathways, borders
Play areas
Lawn or grassy areas
Trees & shrubs
Other plant beds
Water sources
Compost area
North/South/East/West
Gate, other access

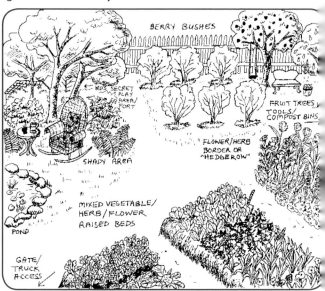

How Much Bounty?

Your food needs will determine the size of your vegetable patch and the planting of fruits (bushes/trees/vines). Additionally, there are other options noted below.

A 100 sq ft Bounty (1-2 people)

Our research proves that growing produce in only 100 sq ft (two 4x12 foot beds) can yield from $30-100+ per month in food, from Spring to Fall. We use all the strategies in this guide! For a small family, 200-400 sq ft (or larger) is an excellent size.

Border Bounty

Increase your yield by planting produce amidst flowers, shrubs, along borders & pathways. *Plant strawberries, lettuce, spinach, kale, cabbage, chard, parsley, radish.*

Vertical Bounty

Use a trellis to increase yield. Place it in part of a bed, alongside a fence or building, or simply use a pole. *Plant pole beans, peas, cucumbers, zuchinni, tomatoes.*

Container Bounty

Pots or durable containers are perfect for a deck, balcony, patio. Be creative! *Plant herbs, greens, tomatoes, peppers, spinach, strawberries, eggplant, even vines like peas or beans* that are trellissed. There are also *fruit trees* created just for growning in a pot!

Natural Environment Factors

Your food garden's yield will be affected by certain factors for which you need to plan, as discussed below. Some are beyond your control while for others you can try to develop practical strategies.

Soil

Your type of soil (sandy, loam, clay) will greatly affect growth and yield. If necessary have it tested for type & pH (page 45) and amend it regularly (Soil Preparation, pp. 12-13). You can also use planting mixes (bagged or bulk) especially created for vegetable gardening

Sun & Shade

Spend time in your garden at various times of the day or season. Identify sun exposure (full, part shade, shade) and length.

Plant maturity is best with at least 8 hours of full sun. Some plants (especially greens) may suffer with hot exposure, so protect them and keep soil slightly moist up to 18 inches deep.

Frost & Wind

Some areas may be susceptible to frost or wind damage. Note this in designing your garden patch. Use protective structures, create a windscreen (fence or shrubs), etc.

Water

Drainage. Identify low spots with poor drainage or sloping land that drains too quickly. Use raised-beds in such locations.

Irrigation. Identify water sources: faucets, sprinkler systems, rain barrels, cisterns, ponds, etc. Determine watering style: hose, overhead sprinkler, soaker hose, drip irrigation, etc.

Storage. Decide if you need/desire to catch and store water. Plan on how you will distribute it to your plants.

Conserve. Use efficient watering methods. Protect water source from poisons, etc.

Garden Ethics

Your garden, whatever size, is a sanctuary. As its keeper strive to make choices that keep it safe, peaceful and beautiful.

Human Friendly. Don't use methods that can harm.

Species Friendly. Use least toxic/harmful strategies.

Earth Friendly. Use, enhance & preserve Nature's resources — especially soil, water, beneficial insects & micro-organisms.

Garden Friendly. Replenish soil, recyle waste, compost, conserve water, use regional & native, non-GMO plants/seeds, and respect the Web of Life that dwells within your garden.

Protection

Scavengers

Predators such as deer, racoons, opossums, moles, gophers, field mice, etc. need to be controlled. Methods range from folklore to commercial. Always use the least toxic method to protect other wildlife, beneficial insects, humans and pets.

Boundary

Food security may require a fence or other means to keep out scavengers, both human & animal!

Harsh Conditions

Use protective structures, such as cloches (p. 23), garden fabrics (i.e. reemay), even an umbrella to protect certain plants from sun, heat, cold, rain, snow, etc.

9

RAISED-BEDS

Elevated methods of agriculture help combat heavy clay or rocky soils, poor drainage, limited space, climate, and terrain issues. In the home garden, raised-beds give a sense of order and ease in planting and maintenance. Intensive planting can also increase yield from 4-10 times over flat ground gardening.

Beyond the initial cost and time to create raised beds, you will find gardening to be easier!

Advantages

- Improved soil quality & tilth
- Very good drainage
- Requires no rototilling
- Soil warms early for Spring planting
- Year-round planting options
- Longer growing season
- Easy watering & fertilizing
- More intensive planting
- Can protect & cover
- Easy for elderly & alter-abled
- All-around easy access

Mounded Beds

Mounded beds are simple to make and can be framed with wood or rocks later. Here's how to do it.

1. **Dig** out an area of grass or soil, say 4x12 feet (48 square feet)
2. **Add** about the same proportions of soil ammendments and fertilizers as for wood/rock beds (see chart, to the right)
3. **Slope** the sides to prevent rain & watering erosion Bed's height will be 6-8 inches, width 3.5 feet
4. **Edge** the base regularly to keep out grass or weeds

Mounded Bed

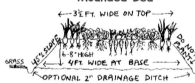

←--- 3½ FT. WIDE ON TOP --→
45°2 SLOPE
6-8" HIGH
4 FT. WIDE AT BASE
DO NOT PLANT!
GRASS
OPTIONAL 2" DRAINAGE DITCH

Design Tips for Wood Beds

- No pressure treated wood or tires (poisonous!)
- Use 2x6, 2x8, 2x10 or 2x12 dimensional lumber
- **Length**: 8-12 feet is ideal (or shorter if small space)
- **Width**: 4-feet (easy reach without stepping into)
- **Height**: minimum 8 inches to 12 inches (best)

Intensive Planting

Raised-beds are perfect for **Intensive Planting** because the depth & quality of the soil is so good. You will be amazed at how much more you can grow in the same amount of space. The most efficient way to plant is in "wide rows" (not single rows that can waste space). This sample layout (4x12 foot bed) is only 48 square feet!

N

2 FT.

←2½ FT.→ ←2½ FT.→
TOMATOES   GARLIC   FENNEL
4 FT. WIDTH
BASIL   MIXED   BROCCOLI   CELERY
CARROTS &
LETTUCE RADISHES
W   E
         CAULIFLOWER   SAGE
MARIGOLDS   PARSLEY

←— EAST/WEST ORIENTATION — 12 FT. LENGTH —→

S

Filling the Raised-Bed

To fill your raised-bed (or to create a mounded-bed,) you will need these ingredients:

- **Sandy Loam** (preferred), or weed-free soil
- **Compost** or other organic matter like leaf mulch
- **Manure** - aged, dry (will not Nitrogen-burn plants)
- **Fertilizers** (organic, to be Earth-friendly)

Don't have any of these? Check your local garden center or outdoor supply store. Bulk or bagged vegetable garden planting mixes are also available that contain compost, manure and fertilizers. Simply add such mixes in the proper quantity to your loam/soil base.

Volume Needed for Main Ingredients of a Raised-Bed

Ingredients	High Bed 4'x12' (48 sq ft) 18 inches high	Low Bed 4'x12' (48 sq ft) 12 inches high	Low Bed 4'x8' (32 sq ft) 12 inches high
Manure (15%)	1/2 cu yd	1/3 cu yd	1/4 cu yd
Compost (35%)	1 cu yd	2/3 cu yd	1/2 cu yd
Sandy Loam (50%)	1.5 cu yd	1 cu yd	3/4 cu yd

- 3-feet clearance on all sides
- Nail long sides out, ends inside
- 10-15 feet from trees
- 18" height for elderly, alter-abled
- Protective covering (page 23)
- East-west placement lengthwise
- Aesthetic integration to garden
- Tiered-bed option

5 Easy Steps

1. Before filling, dig out grass or weeds at bottom of new bed (get out all roots!). A garden fork and shovel work best
2. Add **Sandy Loam** (mix well with any existing soil at bottom of bed)
3. Add **Compost** : mix well with loam
4. Add **Manure** (well-aged): mix well with compost and loam
5. Add **Organic Fertilizers** (see Natural Fertilizers, pp. 14-17): mix well with above loam/compost/manure blend

Voila!
You should now have beautiful, fluffy, dark aerated soil that smells wonderfully rich

Tiered-bed is creative and easy for elderly & kids. Gentle on the back, too!

18" HEIGHT — 4 FT WIDTH

Note: Due to natural compaction and plant ingestion, each gardening season you will need to add perhaps 2-3 inches of compost (or other organic matter) to your raised-bed; add fertilizers as needed.

Protection from Weather
(Cold, wind, heat/sun, young starts, greens)

RIDGEPOLE
FLEXIBLE PVC FRAME
1/2" PVC ARCH SEATS INTO 3/4" PVC PIECES INSIDE BED
METAL BRACKETS
12' 12" 4'

For 4-foot wide beds — Use 8-foot lengths of 1/2" pvc pipes arched over bed, held securely in place and covered with 4-mil clear plastic or Reemay garden fabric

11

SOIL PREPARATION

Every gardener's intent should be to improve the nutrient qual-ity of the soil and its microlife. This is treating the Earth kindly and naturally. Every year the soil in a garden bed needs tending in order for it to "grow" into beautiful tilth that plants crave. How-ever, soil becomes depleted of its nutrients and microlife over the course of a growing season, and because of year-round climatic conditions. Follow these 4 Steps for success.

Creating a new bed? Do all 4 Steps · **Annual fresh-up of a bed? Steps 3 & 4**
Time to balance pH? (its been a few years) **Step 1**

STEP 1   Assess Soil Type & pH

Many crops can be planted as soon as your soil can be worked. But that de-pends on your *soil type,* the quality of its tilth (richness of organic matter) created over time, and oftentimes the height of the bed (raised, mounded, flat).

DO THIS
Determine your soil type:
Clay, Sandy, or Loam.
(See Soil Types, page 45, for details)

Your soil can be tested at a County Extension Service. A soil kit is available at good garden centers. A garden center, club or neighbor might also know your soil type.

The best soil is **LOAM** — a friable (crumbly) mix of sand, silt, clay & decomposed organic matter. You can create incredible loam by fol-lowing the guidelines in this book.

DO THIS
Determine your soil's pH:
Acidity or alkalinity
(see Soil pH, page 45, for details)

Most plants/vegetables prefer slightly acidic soil, from 6.0-6.8. (7.0 is neutral). Potatoes, ber-ries, flowering bulbs like even more acidic soil (5.5-6.0 pH)

A soil test kit can determine pH, as can an Extension office.

Too acidic — add limestone
Too alkaline — add sulphur
(NOTE: *organic matter is best!*)

WHEN TO DO?
New Garden Bed
OR
Amend soil pH
(every 3-4 years)

STEP 2   Prepare Garden Bed: Loosening the Soil

DO THIS

1. Stake out planting area or create raised-bed (see Raised-Beds, pp. 10-11)
2. Dig out any grass or weeds, leav-ing no roots that might resprout
3. Loosen remaining soil, if it is not too wet. A garden fork works well to sift the soil and break up any clods. Never dig wet soil, especially clay types, because it can destroy the soil's structure for up to a year.
4. Now is when you determine if you want to adjust the soil's pH. If so, add proper amount of limestone or sulphur (from Step 1, also page 45), then proceed to Step 3. *Note: Many seasoned gardeners know their soil's needs well and are flexible about pH levels throughout their garden or for different plants.*

STEP 3
Add Soil Amendments

Organic matter — **compost, manure, sandy loam, vegetable planting mix.** These are key to increasing your soil's tilth, texture, nutrients & microlife.

DO THIS:

Annually, mix any of above well into existing soil and with each other. Don't skimp — your bed will compress about 2" in volume over the gardening season. How much to add? See Raised-Beds, pp. 10-11

Using Animal Manures

Best Manures
Rabbit, chicken, duck, goose, llama, alpaca, sheep, goat, birds (all of these have great digestive systems)

Problematic Manures
Cattle/cow (may have high salt content), horse/donkey (weed seeds), pig (parasites/pathogens)

Never Use
Cat, dog, human poop (risk of pathogens, disease, etc.)

Animal manures are suitable as medium release soil amendments containing nitrogen, phosphorous, potassium, and many important trace minerals.

- Manure (fresh) is best added to the compost pile
- If added to the soil directly, manure should be well-aged and you must wait several weeks before planting. Why? Fresh manure has higher Nitrogen levels that can burn plants, unless used sparingly
- It is also possible to add manure (fresh or aged) in Fall in preparation for Spring planting

STEP 4
Add Fertilizers

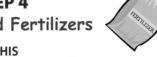

DO THIS
Finally, add Natural Fertilizers on top the prepared soil and mix well, about 4-6 inches deep (use garden fork or shovel)
See Natural Fertilizers, pp. 14-17

Troubleshooting

What would happen if I did not add anything to my soil?
Neglect your soil for a year or two and its mineral content will become depleted. Your crops will show deficiency symptoms and your production will drop. Test your soil, and get back to rebuilding it!

What can I do about poor drainage in my soil?
Adding coarse soil amendments such as sandy loam and compost is important. You may also want to consider using raised-beds.

Can I add manure directly into my soil?
If you do, add the manure in the Fall, if possible, so it will be well broken down by planting time in Spring. If you choose to add it in Spring, use aged manure and try to wait a few weeks before planting, so as to avoid burning of plants.

If my soil is too well-drained, what can I do?
Add plenty of organic matter to your soil to help retain moisture, plant in wide rows, and mulch, mulch, mulch! (See Mulching, pp. 54-57)

If I add compost to my soil do I need anything else?
You will probably need some additional fertilizers for optimal plant production & health. (See Natural Fertilizers, pp. 14-17)

What can I do to protect my soil from winter rain and snow?
You can either mulch your soil under a thick layer of leaves, straw or ground cloth; grow fall/winter vegetables if your winters are mild; or cover crop with any of a number of cold-hardy legumes or grains.

NATURAL FERTILIZERS
Balancing & Enriching Soil

Most gardeners know the value of periodic additions of fertilizer to the soil both to enrich it and to balance such vital minerals as nitrogen (N), phosphorous (P), potassium (K), calcium, magnesium and sulfur that get depleted. Amending the soil should be a dedicated part of gardening.

SAVE the PLANET
Fertilizers:
Natural
vs
Synthetic

Boxed, liquid or bulk varieties of both natural and synthetic fertilizers are available. Please make a choice that benefits Earth — buy natural (or make your own blend)!

Natural fertilizers are **not** created in a laboratory. They are found in the ocean, plants, rocks and animals. Thus, they are rich in trace minerals and nutrients that release slowly, from 6 months to 5 years.

The insoluable quality of a natural fertilizer allows a plant to "store-and-use" as needed. Such fertilizers stimulate growth of micro-life and earthworms. They help create friable soil, minimize water contamination, and create optimal nutrient content and more flavor in produce.

Synthetic chemical fertilizers are so potent and unnatural that they kill off much of the microbial life in the soil. Their high acid salt content also burns through the soil, unbalancing its mineral content and microlife. Furthermore, synthetic fertilizers are created to "force-feed" the plant quickly (with high Nitrogen doses), for faster results, at the expense of the soil's health. Finally, such fertilizers, often being high in nitrogen, are a leading cause of groundwater, aquifer and water runoff contamination.

What's N-P-K?

Most fertilizers sold commercially will have a N-P-K ratio listed on the label, such as 4-6-2 or 7-7-7, or 10-5-1, etc. These numbers refer to the percentage amount available of the macro-nutrients (N)Nitrogen, (P)Phosphorous, & (K) Potassium.

Nitrogen is vital for overall development of stems and leaves. **Caution**: too much causes excess growth at the expense of fruit and flower production.

Phosphorous is vital for good root production and, very importantly, for seed germination, flowering, and setting of fruit.

Potassium is vital in promoting general vigor, including disease, heat and cold resistance. It is also key to the turgor (uprightness) of stems and thickness of cell walls.

Other key minerals for plant and soil health are Calcium, Magnesium and Sulfur.

TIP! Read the Label

A synthetic fertilizer (the big seller at stores) often has significant Nitrogen content, plus unlisted inert ingredients. You should want full disclosure.

A natural fertilizer mix is fairly tame and balanced, with all ingredients listed.

2 GREAT USES!

Plants, weather and disease deplete soil of its needed energy. Also, while growing, plants appreciate a little boost of energy. In both cases, natural fertilizers are beneficial.

Soil Amendment
(see page 17 for details)

Intermix fertilizer thoroughly into soil in Spring, when creating a new bed, or before planting.

Sidedressing
(see pp. 26-27 for details)
Sprinkle around plants

Make Your Own Natural Fertilizer Blend

Commercial slow-release organic fertilizer mixes are widely available, but you can make your own to meet your specific needs plus save money! A well-stocked garden center may have individual ingredients in bulk so that you can create custom mixes/blends.
We created the following balanced blends and have successfully used them for many years.

Blend #1: NPK 2-5-3   *Long-release Period*

1 part bloodmeal
2 parts rock phosphate
2 parts seaweed
3 parts greensand

You might also need to add compost initially and/or an additional nitrogen source after 6-8 wks, otherwise very long-lived (5 years)

Blend #2: NPK 2-10-2   *Phosphorous Boost*

2 parts cottonseed meal
2 parts rock phosphate
2 parts greensand

Especially good for root crops flowering bulbs, & berries (all need lots of phosphorous)

Blend #3: NPK 2.5-5.5-2.5 *Effective All-purpose*

2 parts cottonseed meal
1 part colloidal phosphate
2 parts granite dust

Good all-purpose fertilizer; you can increase the cotton-seed meal to boost N %

Blend #4: (calculated by weight for 100 sq ft)   *All-purpose Boost*

3# alfalfa meal
1# bloodmeal
2# bonemeal
5# colloidal phosphate
1/2# kelp meal
10# greensand

This blend contains fast & slow release forms of NPK plus trace minerals. Excel-lent for cooler weather, de-pleted soil or first time gar-deners. The second year add only nitrogen or maybe 2 tablespoons bonemeal per plant when you plant

Note: None of these mixes contain Lime because that would limit the versatility of their use

Balanced & Safe

The possibility of overdosing or burning your crops is slight with slow-release organic fertilizers. Exceptions are bloodmeal (fast release and high nitrogren content) and kelp meal (has potent growth hormones (see chart, next page).

Fertilizers can be measured and added separately to plants (sidedressing), but mixes also create "balanced" and "complete" releases when they are turned well into the soil at planting time. Finally, no mix will successfully replace the need for yearly additions of organic matter (compost, leaf mulch, etc.) to your garden soil — about 2-3 inches worth.

15

Soil Macronutrients: A Quick Reference Guide

Nutrient & Function	Natural Sources (in powdered form)	N-P-K/Trace Minerals (T)		Use per 100 sq ft.
Nitrogen ("N") Stimulates vegetative development and is vital to the growth of stems & leaves (too much causes excess growth at the expense of fruit & flower production)	Alfalfa Meal	5-1-2	T	2.5 to 5 lbs
	Animal manures	varies	T	varies with type/age
	Bloodmeal	13-1.5-.6		1-2 lbs
	Compost	2.5-1-1.5	T	2 in + annually
	Cottonseed meal	5-2.5-1.6		5-10 lbs
	Crabmeal	10-.25-.05	T	2-5 lbs
	Fish emulsion (liquid)	5-1-1	T	1-3 Tbs/gal water
	Fish meal	10-6-0	T	2-5 lbs
	Seaweed	1-0-1	T	Foliar spray
	Soybean meal	6.5-1.5-2.4		5-10 lbs
	Fava beans (cover crop)			1-2 lb of seed
	Crimson clover	2-.5-2		1/4 lb of seed
	Austrian field peas	2.5-0-1		1-2 lbs of seed
Phosphorous ("P") Relates to good root production & also strongly influences fruiting & flowering. Very important in seed germination & metabolism of seedlings	Bonemeal (steamed)	1 to 7-20-0		2-5 lbs
	Colloidal phosphate	0-18-0	T	7.5 lbs
	Rock phosphate	0-33-0	T	5-10 lbs
Potassium ("K") Promotes general vigor; disease, heat & cold resistance; and relates to turgor (uprightness) of stems & thickness of cell walls	Kelp meal	1-0-12	T	1 lb
	Liquid seaweed	1.7-.8-5	T	Foliar spray
	Greensand	0-1.5-5		10-25 lbs
	Granite dust	0-0-3 to 6		20 lbs
Calcium Ingredient of cell walls concerned with the development of roots & growing stem points	Agricultural lime, or	96% calcium		5-20 lbs (depends on soil type & pH)
	Dolomite lime (if soil pH is too low)	46% calcium 46 % magnesium		same as above
	Gypsum (if soil pH too high)	22% calcium 17% sulfur		1 lb
	Bonemeal (see above)	30% calcium		
Magnesium Relates to chlorophyll production & the catylization of most enzyme reactions	Dolomite lime (raises pH; use only if your soil needs calcium and magnesium, otherwise use agricultural lime)	46% magnesium 46% calcium		5-20 lbs (depends on soil type & pH)
Sulfur Used in production of plant protein, plant metabolism, & formation of chlorophyl	Sulfur	100% sulfur		1/2 to 2 lbs
	Gypsum (see above)	22% calcium 17% sulfur		(depends on pH) use 1 lb

16

3-5 months
2 years
5-8 weeks
1-2 years
1-6 months
4-6 months

10-14 days
4-6 months

4-6 months

turned under
at bloom from
2-6 months

6 months
3 years
5 years

4-6 months
short-term
5 years
3-5 years

3-4 years

3-4 years

1 year

3-4 years

1 year
1 year
1 year

IMPORTANT USE!
Natural Fertilizer as Soil Amendment

The nutritional value of produce is dependent upon nutrient-rich soil. A plant draws these nutrients into itself. However, the soil gets depleted and must be "amended" with more minerals and microlife from compost, cover crops and natural fertilizers.

The chart shows that there are alternate choices in determining which source to use for what macronutrient. Notice that the minerals have from short- (see Nitrogen) to long-term *effective release times*. Over time, you will develop preferences for certain sources.

When gardening, it is helpful to keep records of when you work the soil and amend it. This will help determine when to fertilize and/or amend the soil the next time.

3 Ways to Amend Soil with a Natural Fertilizer
- Select and add individual *natural sources* (see chart), **or**
- Add a complete mix/blend (commercial or homemade), **or**
- Add a balanced vegetable garden planting mix (bagged or bulk available from a garden or outdoor supply center — these are generally well-balanced)

When to Amend Soil?
Spring • Creating a New Bed • Before Planting

Step 1
Spade (use shovel and/or a garden fork) to loosen up the top 8-10 inches of soil.

Step 2
Mix organic matter (compost, leaf mulch, or garden planting mix, if desired) and any necessary fertilizers into the top 4-6 inches. Blend #4 (p. 15) is good to use.

Step 3 Moisten soil thoroughly; plant seeds or starts.

learn **HOW TO SIDEDRESS** pp. 26-27

17

COMPANION PLANTING

One of gardening's joys is to discover ways that plants benefit each other when interplanted. A diversely planted vegetable garden intermixes crops, herbs & flowers. You can enhance the happy life of your vegetables & fruits by knowing what companions they enjoy sharing space with. Such "arranged marriages" are easy to integrate into your garden design.

Companion Planting:
Strength
in Diversity

Companion planting helps create a strong community of plants, the diversity of which has numerous benefits:

Pest Control
Certain plants repel or confuse insect & animal pests. Companion plants may also attract beneficial insects that aid in pollination or feed on insect pests.

Soil Enhancement
Certain plants add specific nutrients to the soil that are needed by surrounding plants (example: Legumes fixate nitrogen into the soil).

Weed Control
Beneficial interplantings can aid in keeping weeds down under larger plants or around fruit trees, vines, etc.

Erosion Control
Soil is stabilized by providing dense, water absorbant root structures. Soil is not left barren, unprotected.

Plant Protection & Support
Taller plants may protectively shade shorter neighbors from excess sun. Stronger plants can support weaker ones.

Plant Yield & Flavor
More yield is available by planting more intensively. Some plants improve the flavor of others.

Is It Necessary?

There are numerous tricks in creating a more productive and aesthetic garden. Companion planting is one technique. Why?

• You can cram more plants into a smaller space — plants that like each other and work to insure health & safety among neighbors.
• You can intermix herbs, flowers & vegetables, thereby creating more interest and edible harvest.
• You can thin interplantings to keep proper balance between growth, productivity & support

Companion planting mixes scientific fact, function & aesthetics. Try it and you won't turn back!

GARLIC
CABBAGE
NASTURTIUM

STEP 2:

Space-Efficient Root Growth

These combinations have root systems that will not compete with each other, thus root space is used efficiently.

Beans	— carrots, celery, corn, squash
Corn	— lettuce, potatoes, squash
Kohlrabi	— beets
Leeks	— carrots
Lettuce	— carrots, onions, radishes
Melons	— radishes
Onions	— eggplants, peppers, radishes, spinach
Parsnips	— lettuce
Peas	— radishes or turnips
Chard	— cucumbers

Interplanting: 3 Easy Steps

STEP 1:   Avoid Incompatible Plants

Certain plants just do not benefit each other. They emit growth-stunting chemicals or attract diseases in their neighbors. Don't plant these vegetables near each other:

DON'T PLANT TOMATOES near ...

Cabbage Family:
broccoli, cabbage, kale, cauliflower, kohlrabi, brussel sprouts **(stunts growth)**

Potatoes (draws blight)

Corn (attracts corn earworm)

Beans, peas, legumes AVOID
Onion, garlic shallots, chives (both stunt each others growth)

Beets AVOID Pole beans (both stunt each others growth)

Plant Space-Compatible Vegetables

CORN
POLE BEANS
SQUASH

Compatible Top-Growth

These varieties grow well together because they have above-ground growth patterns that don't interfer — high growers mixed with low growers.

Beans — celery, corn, squash, radishes, or staked tomatoes

Broccoli, — carrots, onions, trellised peas, carrots, onions, peppers,
Cauliflower   squash, tomatoes, corn
& Cabbage

Leeks — carrots, parsley

Lettuce — carrots, onions, radishes

Melons — radishes, corn, cabbage

Onions — cabbage, carrots, eggplant, peppers, spinach

Peas — broccoli, cauliflower, cabbage, turnips, lettuce, carrots,
(trellised)   spinach, kohlrabi, radishes

Potatoes — corn or pumpkins (Combinations of potatoes and corn and pumpkins take lots of nutrients from the soil, so be careful!)

Step 3: Know Insect Repelling Herbs — this way

STEP 3:   Plant Insect-Repelling Herbs & Flowers

Plants produce four major chemical substances (see below) that aid in survival. By intermixing the proper varieties of plants, the predator-prey relationship between insects will be balanced such that you may need little or no outside help with sprays, dusts, and the like.

Attractant - draws insects toward the plant
Stimulant - encourages insects to feed or lay eggs
Deterrent - inhibits insects from feeding or laying their eggs
Repellent - drives insects away

Herbs for Interplanting

Herb	Insects & Pests Repelled
Basil	Asparagus beetle, fly, mosquito, tomato hornworm
Castor Bean	Sometimes deters moles, rats & other rodents, mosquito, nematode
Catnip *	Aphid, Colorado potato beetle, cucumber beetle, flea beetle, Japanese beetle, squash bug
Dill	Cabbage looper, imported cabbage worm, tomato hornworm
Fennel *	Aphid, slug & snail
Garlic	Aphid, cabbage looper, cabbage maggot, codling moth, cabbageworm, Japanese beetle, peachborer, even rabbits!
Geranium	Cabbageworm, corn earworm, leafhopper
Nasturtium	Aphid, cabbage looper, Colorado potato beetle, cucumber beetle, whitefly, cabbage worm, squash bug *(nasturtiums can attract black aphids)*
Onion	Cabbage looper, carrot fly, Colorado potato beetle, cabbageworm, rabbits
Parsley	Asparagus beetle
Peppermint *	Ant, aphid, cabbage looper, flea beetle, cabbageworm, squash bug, whitefly, white cabbage moth
Spearmint *	Aphid, cabbage looper, flea beetle, squash bug
Sage *	Cabbage looper, cabbage maggot, carrot fly, cabbageworm
Thyme *	Cabbage looper, cabbageworm, whitefly
Wormwood *(Artemisia)*	Ant, cabbage looper, cabbage maggot, carrot fly, codling moth, flea beetle, field mouse & possibly other animals, whitefly

*perennial   (Note: catnip, mints, sages can be very vigorous, so control their growth!

KEY: Plant herbs & flowers between rows/plants or as hedgerow

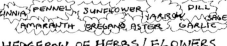

ZINNIA FENNEL SUNFLOWER DILL
AMARANTH OREGANO ASTER YARROW SAGE GARLIC

HEDGEROW OF HERBS / FLOWERS
AT BACK OR SIDE OF GARDEN

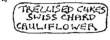

TRELLISED CUKES
SWISS CHARD
CAULIFLOWER

TRELLISED PEAS
BROCCOLI
SPINACH + RADISHES

POTATOES
BEANS
CELERY

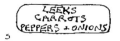

LEEKS
CARROTS
PEPPERS + ONIONS

Diversify Plantings

If you plant *too many crops from one family in the same area*, your chances of problems increase.

SOLUTION — **Companion Planting** (see pp. 18-20). Very simply, plant crops from two or more families close together or intermixed, and add an herb or two.   *See sample plot.*

Crop Rotation

Crop rotation (an important farming method) is one of the best ways a gardener can prevent plant disease and minimize insect pest problems (or at least confuse their raging appetites!). Additionally, it can help restore or sustain nutrients in the soil so that it does not get exhausted.

The General Rule: Don't plant the same crop in the same place all the time! Rotate plants from other families into that location over the course of 1-2 years.

Familiarity with the various plant families (see list), each of whose members share the same vulnerabilities, will help you work out a sensible rotation that works for you. Experiment!

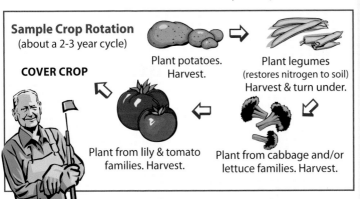

Sample Crop Rotation
(about a 2-3 year cycle)

COVER CROP

Plant potatoes. Harvest.

Plant legumes (restores nitrogen to soil) Harvest & turn under.

Plant from cabbage and/or lettuce families. Harvest.

Plant from lily & tomato families. Harvest.

Sample Rotation (for very poor soil)
1. Cover crop first (see pp. 50-53)
2. Plant corn & squash (big soil depleters). Harvest.
3. Plant legumes (to restore nitrogen to soil). Harvest, turn under.
4. Plant from cabbage family (include garlic). Harvest.
5. Plant from carrot & lettuce families. Harvest, cover crop.

Sample Garden Plot of Intermixed Plant Families

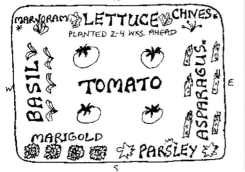

MARJORAM LETTUCE CHIVES
PLANTED 2-4 WKS. AHEAD
N
BASIL
TOMATO
ASPARAGUS
E
W
MARIGOLD
PARSLEY
S

Saving Seeds?

If you plan to save your own seed, remember that members within a family can cross-pollinate, resulting in possible plant mutations.

SOLUTION Isolate plants from each other as much as possible, or cover during pollination when flowers are open.

21

SPRING PLANTING

Know Dates of Last Frost

Most gardeners plant new seeds and young starts in Spring. It is possible to get a successful jump on the gardening season by following at least 5 strategies, as shown on these two pages. The result will be a quicker harvest while making the most of the frost-free growing days in your area.

You should know if your area is susceptible to frost and when. A local garden center or County Extension Service (even garden club or fellow gardener) can tell you these two dates:

- **Last Frost Date in Spring**
- **First Frost Date in Fall**

Last Frost Dates vary greatly from place to place (or even from yard to yard). The following charts are a general guide for Spring. Always be prepared to

protect your seeds and starts from harsh weather.

STRATEGY #2
Know Your Soil's Temperature
for Seed Germination

Soil temperature must be above 40F for seeds to successfully germinate (or they may rot in the cool/moist soil). Direct seeding at higher temperatures will result in faster sprouting.

A soil thermometer (widely available) will give you an accurate reading. Use the following *minimum to maximum soil temperatures* as a guide for planting.

Range: 40-70F+
Onions, Parsnip, Spinach

Range: 50-80F+
Asparagus, Beets, Cabbage family, Carrot, Cauliflower, Celery, Chard, Lettuce, Parsley, Peas, Potatoes, Radishes, Turnips

Range: 60-85F+
Beans, Corn, Cucumber, Eggplant, Lima beans, Melons, Okra, Peppers Pumpkin, Squash, Zuchinni

Semi-Hardy

Plant as early as 2 weeks **before** average last frost date, or use your own garden records.

Cauliflower
Potatoes

Hardy Crops

Plant as soon as soil can be worked in Spring. In marginal weather conditions, protect with a cloche, light insulating fabric. Be creative!

Artichoke	Herbs
Asparagus	Mustard
Beets	Onions
Berries	Parsnips
Broccoli	Peas
Cabbage	Herbs
Celery	Radishes
Chard	Rhubarb
Cover crops	Spinach
Garlic	Perennial
Kale	flowers

Very Tender

Plant at least 2 weeks or more **after** average last Spring frost date unless there is a clear warming trend earlier, or you live in southern climates.

Basil	Cucumber
Eggplant	Lima Beans
Melons	Okra
Peppers	Pumpkins
Squash	

Tender Crops

Plant one week or so after date of last Spring frost. Be cautious, however, and be prepared to protect.

Beans	Herbs
Sweet corn	Tomatoes

STRATEGY #3
Have Good Drainage

Raised or mounded beds have excellent drainage. This allows them to warm up earlier in the Spring and stay warm later in the Fall.

Flat ground gardening may not have proper drainage. A proper solution is the addition of 2-3" compost/organic matter once a year. See Strategy #4

STRATEGY #4 Add Organic Matter

In Spring (or Fall, if desired)

1. Add 2-3 inches of compost, well-aged manure, or garden vegetable planting soil mix. *Note: remove any mulch from the soil first*

2. Add some natural fertilizers, if desired or necessary (see pp.14-17).

3. Mix into the soil well, 6-10 inches.

This is an important part of **Soil Preparation** (see pp. 12-13), especially in Spring when soil temperatures are cool.

Nitrogen and phosphorous are locked up in the soil, unavailable to plants, when the soil temperature is below 50F. Then, as the days get longer, the sun shines more, and the soil gradually warms up, the young plants will be able to take advantage of the soil nutrients as soon as they are released.

Mistake #1

Don't plant hot weather crops too soon, or you risk stunting them — Tomatoes, peppers, eggplant, beans, corn, squash, cucumber

Mistake #2

Never walk directly on your garden beds, especially raised beds. This severely compacts the soil. Create beds no wider than 4-feet, for easy reach.

Mistake #3

Don't plant seeds if the soil temperature is below 40F — they will not germinate. Direct-seeding at higher soil temperatures results in faster germination.

Mistake #4

Don't plant starts or seeds too soon if there is the likelihood of frost. Know frost dates for your area and have the means to protect young plants.

STRATEGY #5   Protect Your Plants

Cloche

Made from clear plastic or glass, a cloche easily protects seeds, starts & soil in a cold spell. Cloches can be bought, but the method below is useful for 4-foot wide wood raised or mounded beds. Use 8-foot lengths of 1/2" pvc pipes arched over bed, held securely in place and covered with 4-mil clear plastic.

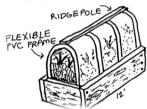

RIDGEPOLE

FLEXIBLE PVC FRAME

12'

12"

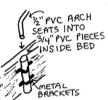

1/2" PVC ARCH SEATS INTO 3/4" PVC PIECES INSIDE BED

METAL BRACKETS

Floating Row Cover

Reemay is a light, white, gauze-like fabric that has high insulation value. It is laid over seed beds or seedlings until warm weather arrives. Each layer blocks 20% of the sun's rays but still allows water & air to pass through. A sheet of light plastic can also be used.

HELD DOWN BY ROCKS

Cold Frame

A simple wooden box with an old window hinged on top is a perfect miniature greenhouse with ventilation. Excellent for hardening-off young starts for a couple weeks before planting in garden bed.

RAISING & PLANTING STARTS

Many gardeners confidently raise their plants from seeds directly sown in the ground, or from purchased starts. You can also raise your own transplants (starts) indoors from seed, about 1-2 months before you expect to place them in your garden. Here are 7 valuable steps.

Step 1: *Containers*

Creatively use containers that drain well with holes in the bottom: small plastic tubs, cups or pots, egg or milk cartons, tin cans, aluminum or commercial planting trays. A plant should grow from seed to full transplant size without being root-bound.

- "Jiffy pellet" pots (at garden centers, 2x2-inch size)) are excellent for growing transplants. When ready, place the pot and its seedling in the ground to minimize transplant shock to the roots.
- Seedling too big for its pot? Transplant it right away or repot into larger container
- Peppers, eggplants, tomatoes, etc. can be grown in 1-gallon or larger containers until plants are quite large and ready to be transplanted

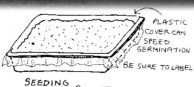

PLASTIC COVER CAN SPEED GERMINATION

BE SURE TO LABEL

SEEDING

TO THIN OUT, SNIP OFF STEMS AT SOIL LINE WITH SMALL, SHARP SCISSORS

THINNING

Step 2: *Sowing Seeds*

Use a sterile soil or non-soil mix (at garden centers) for high success rate of seed germination. Premoisten the soil mix.

1. Scatter seeds over the soil surface or in rows. Plant larger seeds one at a time. Cover seeds with soil mix.
2. If soil is premoistened before seeding and containers are covered with saran wrap or placed in a plastic bag, you may not need to water again until shoots emerge, then . . .
3. Remove plastic and place trays or pots in bright south or east facing window, or place under grow lights. Thin as necessary.

Step 3: *Temperature*

For germination of seeds, warm soil (75-80F) is best

For best plant growth after seeds sprout —
Daytime: 68-70F;
Nighttime: 52-60F

A simple coldframe. The hinged top is an old window. A perfect mini-greenhouse!

Step 4: *Light*

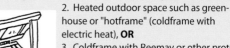

A sunny, south-facing window works fine in areas where the sun shines a lot. In regions with cloudy/rainy springs, transplants will be leggy and weak unless you try this:

1. Indoor grow lights (an expensive but efficient option), **OR**
2. Heated outdoor space such as greenhouse or "hotframe" (coldframe with electric heat), **OR**
3. Coldframe with Reemay or other protective fabric over plants. This may suffice for later planting or in milder climates

Step 5: *Watering*

- *Before seeding, soil mix should be moist.* Perlite, vermiculite or sphagnum peat moss added to the soil are excellent water-absorbing mediums *(Note: Soil mixes may already have these)*
- *Use declorinated water* by setting a jug of tap water out overnight without a lid; keep water at room temperature
- *The right moisture level of the soil is critical.* Too moist and seeds won't germinate, or seedlings can die from "damping-off", a fungus disease. So, while "moist", soil should also feel somewhat crumbly.
- Once up, *plants may have to be watered every day*. Do not allow plants to dry out.

Step 6: *Fertilizing*

Indoor seedlings (starts).
When 2-4 true leaves appear, apply liquid fertilizer (1/2 normal strength) every 1-2 weeks to soil surface. Premixed liquid fertilizers are available at garden centers. Homemade compost tea is good, too.

Direct seeding or planting larger starts (store bought) in garden.
If you prepared the soil properly, you will not need to fertilize until sidedressing (see Sidedressing pp. 26-27).

Step 7: *Hardening Off*

At least 2 weeks before transplanting, starts need to be "hardened-off" because their protection indoors has made them too tender for the garden.

Put starts in a closed coldframe (insulated, if necessary) and open the lid gradually over time. This allows the plants to become strong and resilient for transplanting. *(Note: a greenhouse, cloche, or protected porch may also work)*

Planting New Starts & Seeds

Starts and seeds should be planted after soil is prepped and during early morning, late afternoon, or on a cloudy day — never in the heat of the day!

Planting starts (should have 2-4 true leaves)
1. Water the start before transplanting (to keep rootball intact)
2. Scoop out soil in garden bed (with trowel) about twice the size and depth of rootball, then place start (or Jiffy-potted seedling), firm soil around it and water
3. *Option: Fertilize* (Step 6 above) if soil has not been amended with fertilizer
4. Keep newly planted start out of direct sun for at least 24 hrs and keep soil moist!

Direct planting of seeds: broadcast or plant in rows; poke seeds in ground or scatter; cover with 1/4 - 1-inch of soil (see seed packet); keep soil moist; may protect with garden fabric until seedlings emerge (or have 2-4 true leaves)

Vegetables to Transplant
(approx. weeks after sowing seed indoors)

Broccoli	5-7 wks	Lettuce	5-7
Brussel Sprouts	5-7	Leeks	8-10
Cabbages	5-7	Onion	8-10
Cauliflower	5-7	Parsley	8-10
Celery	7-12	Peppers	6-8
Collards	5-7	Tomatoes	6-8
Eggplant	6-8		

Transplant these plants without disturbing roots. Best if started in individual pots:

Cantaloupe	3-4 wks
Corn	4-6
Cucumbers	3-4
Squashes	3-4
Watermelon	5-7

Succession Planting
Want to extend your harvest of a particular crop? Use this gardening technique! **First**, save some unplanted space in your vegetable patch — this is important. **Second**, plant the same crop more than once (2-4 weeks apart) in those unplanted spaces. Use saved extra seeds, or buy new starts. This technique is great for planting peas, beans, greens (spinach, lettuce, chard, arugala, etc.). Experiment!

HOW TO SIDEDRESS

When you add fertilizers to your soil *after the plants are already growing and in place* — say, midway through the growing season — the process is called "sidedressing." Not all of your plants will need this extra boost. It depends on when and how you last fertilized them. The chart below may help you decide. Then select one or more ways to fertilize, as shown to the right.

What & When To Sidedress

Crop	When to Fertilize + Amount
Brassicas * (broccoli, cabbage, brussel sprouts)	1 TBS — When head first begins to form
Cauliflower	1-2 TBS — When leaves seem full grown but before head begins to form (5-6 wks after transplanting)
Corn *	1 TBS — When knee high and again when it starts to tassle and form silks on stalks
Greens * (lettuce, chard, spinach, mustard)	After trimming half of your crop at a time down to 1 inch or so, or mid-season, use this: A handful of composted manure per sq ft, or a very light dusting of bloodmeal or fish meal or some fish emulsion (2 Tbs/gal of water) poured around base of plants or foliar spray
Leeks	When about 8-12 inches tall, mound compost or aged manure around each
Onions *	When 6-8" tall and every 2 weeks until bulbs begin to expand (the bigger the green tops, the bigger the bulb!), add 3 cups complete fertilizer per 4x4' wide row
Peas & Beans	Usually don't need sidedressing
Potatoes *	1 TBS — 6-7 weeks after planting when plants start to blossom and before hilling for the last time
Summer squash & Zucchini *	1-2 TBS — When first flowers appear
Tomatoes, Peppers Okra, Eggplants	1 TBS — At blossom time or just as very first fruits are starting to form
Vine Crops * (melons, cucumbers, winter squash)	1 TBS — Fertilize before vines start to spread out, when plants are still upright & compact

* Designates heavy feeders requiring a little extra nitrogen

4 WAYS TO SIDEDRESS

IMPORTANT USE!

#1: Fertilize around the drip line

The outside edge of the leaf or branch spread of the plant, and beyond, is called the drip line. Why? Nutrients & water are absorbed in one specific place — the 1/100 inch tip end of the root!

#2: Single-row planting

If you planted neat & tidy rows, fertilize **between** the rows to cover maximum root area

#3: Wide-row planting

Broadcast, sprinkle, or spray your fertilizer over the entire area planted with a certain crop

#4: FOLIAR SPRAY

Foliar sprays permeate the cells of leaves and stems, mostly bypassing the soil. They are available (both organic and synthetic) at garden centers.

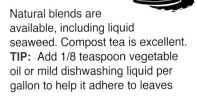

"Miracle Gro" is perhaps the most famous synthetic foliar spray that stimulates too rapid of growth. Don't use it!

Natural blends are available, including liquid seaweed. Compost tea is excellent.
TIP: Add 1/8 teaspoon vegetable oil or mild dishwashing liquid per gallon to help it adhere to leaves

Compost Tea:
Perfect Homemade Sidedressing

Known as **Liquid Gold**, compost tea is a liquid version of compost that acts as a very mild, organic liquid fertilizer usable any time of year.

You can buy it in bulk or make some simply & cheaply at home:

- Add to a bucket: 1/3 fresh compost and 2/3 water
- Steep & stir regularly 3-4 days
- Strain mixture through porous fabric
- Dilute liquid with water (10 parts water to one part compost tea)
- **Use immediately!** Apply to soil or as foliar spray

27

The Nutrition Connection
Reduce Cancer Risk

The National Cancer Institute estimates that about 30-60% of all cancers are linked with diet. Many medical practitioners suggest that persons with high fruit & vegetable intake have about half the risk of cancer than those with low intakes. Makes you want to garden!

The American Cancer Society's 10-step program suggests several strategies directly related to what you can grow and harvest from your garden (or benefit from good produce selection in a store).

You can also reduce cancer risk by eating less fats & salts, minimizing alcohol, drugs & smoking, protecting your skin from the sun, and making a regular commitment to exercise & weight control.

Strategy 1: Cruciferous vegetables (cabbage family)
Plant broccoli, cauliflower, brussels sprouts, all cabbages & kale — all exceptionally nutritious vegetables

Strategy 2: Choose foods rich in vitamin A
Use this rule of thumb: ***the brighter the orange or darker the green, the higher the vitamin A content.*** Plant carrots, squash, a peach or apricot tree, leafy vegetables such as chard, spinach, collards, kale, mustard greens, dark loose-leaf lettuces, parsley, endive, and of course, broccoli

Strategy 3: Choose foods with vitamin C
Grow fresh fruits & vegetables such as grapefruit, kiwi, cantaloupe, oranges, strawberries, red & green peppers, broccoli, tomatoes, winter squash

Strategy 4: Add more high-fiber foods
Include in your diet more fruits & vegetables including peaches, strawberries, potatoes, spinach, tomatoes, greens

Cancer Threats	Eat More
Colon & Prostrate	cruciferous vegetables, carrots, & soybean products
Breast	as above + items high in vitamin C
Lung	dark green leafy & cruciferous vegies, yellow or orange produce, especially carrots
Bladder	fruits & vegetables in general, especially carrots
Throat types	all fruits & vegetables
Thyroid	cruciferous vegetables (cabbage family)
Pancreatic	citrus fruit, tomatoes, legumes

Note: As always, seek the advice of a medical professional if you intend to make a significant change in your diet and/or exercise patterns

The Basics of Nutrition

A garden is a nutritious cornucopia. It can aid immensely in the shaping of your diet, allowing optimal ingestion of beneficial vitamins, minerals, fiber, protein and water, while supplying lower amounts of carbohydrates, calories, fat, and sodium. Dollar for dollar, pound for pound, your garden is a valuable investment in your health!

The Power of Nutrients

The trillions of cells of your body are formed directly from the nutrients in the foods you eat daily. The term *nutrients* describes the chemical elements & compounds in food that aid in cell-building and use of energy. Cell-building materials come from protein, carbohydrates & minerals. Energy-giving components are measured in calories and are obtained from carbohydrates & fat (if these are in short supply, the body can use protein for energy). If too few calories are available, your body may not have enough energy to function properly; too many and the excess is stored as fat.

Most nutrients, acting in chemical enzymes, have a variety of specific tasks, yet they work together in many different combinations to handle the work of the body. A balanced diet assures an available supply of all nutrients and other food components, including fiber.

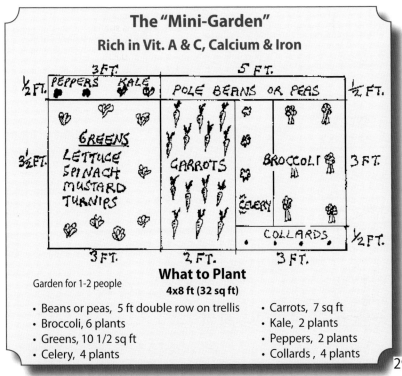

The "Mini-Garden"
Rich in Vit. A & C, Calcium & Iron

PEPPERS KALE — POLE BEANS OR PEAS

GREENS
LETTUCE
SPINACH
MUSTARD
TURNIPS

CARROTS

BROCCOLI

CELERY

COLLARDS

3 FT. — 2 FT. — 3 FT.

½ FT. — 3½ FT. — 3 FT. — ½ FT.

What to Plant
4x8 ft (32 sq ft)

Garden for 1-2 people

- Beans or peas, 5 ft double row on trellis
- Broccoli, 6 plants
- Greens, 10 1/2 sq ft
- Celery, 4 plants
- Carrots, 7 sq ft
- Kale, 2 plants
- Peppers, 2 plants
- Collards , 4 plants

29

The Nutrition Connection
The Power of Greens

Dark Green Leafy Vegetables *(the darker the green, the more the vitamin A!)*, especially chard, spinach, collards, kale, mustard greens & broccoli sit at the top of the list of the *most nutritious vegetables* you can grow, even in a small space, as the design below demonstrates.

Green Nutrition

- *Romaine lettuce* has 3x the vit. C & 6x the vit. A of iceberg lettuce, and provides more iron, calcium & other nutrients
- *Endive* contains 5x the vit. A of head lettuce & 3x the calcium & iron
- *Dark green looseleaf lettuces* have more vit. A than crisp or butterhead varieties
- *Young unsprayed dandelion greens* are rich in vit. A & iron, eaten raw or cooked

- *Parsley* is one of the most nutritious greens, high in vit. A & C, and iron
- *Collards* (one serving) supplies more than the U.S. RDA of vit. A & C plus important amounts of iron, calcium, B vitamins, & some protein

Fantastic Fruits!

Cantaloupes Of all the fruits typically eaten in the U.S., this may be the most nutritious. One quarter cantaloupe provides nearly a full day's supply of vit. A & C.

Watermelons are very nutritious as well.

Citrus fruits (oranges, grapefruit, etc.), tomatoes, strawberries, kiwi, & honeydew melons are all high in vit. C.

Apples, grapes & plums, while less vitamin-rich, still have valuable fiber.

And of course, all fruit are full of natural occuring water!

Salad Garden

2 FT.	4 FT.	
KALE KALE	2½ FT. APART IN CAGES	
GREENS	SALAD TOMATO	CHERRY TOMATO
LETTUCE SPINACH MUSTARD		
	SWEET PEPPER	GREEN ONIONS	CARROTS
	PARSLEY	CHIVES	

1 FT. 1 FT. 2 FT.

What to Plant
4'x6' (24 sq ft)

- Peppers, 2 plants
- Cherry tomato, 1 plant
- Salad tomato, 1 plant
- Greens, 8 sq ft
- Kale or chard, 2 plants
- Carrots, 4 sq ft widerow
- Green onions, 2 sq ft
- Chives, 1 clump
- Parsley, 1-2 plants

Garden for 1-2 people

Note: This intensively planted garden is perfect for raised or mounded bed

From Soil to Plant to Person:
Cultivating Health & Nutrition

There are 23 mineral elements needed for human health that come from the soil and are converted by plants, along with carbon, hydrogen, & oxygen, into food nutrients — amino acids, carbohydrates, essential fats, vitamins, minerals, enzymes, & fiber. A deficiency of even one element in our food will eventually lead to health problems in our body.

When plants are grown properly in nutrient-rich soil their absorption of these 23 mineral nutrients can be maximized, boosting the nutrition of the food. In turn, as we ingest the nutrients (i.e. minerals & vitamins) in food, our bodies use them in thousands of enzymes. Acting as little chemical sparkplugs, these enzymes drive our body's huge engine of metabolism — every vital function of the body to keep alive — and each minute of every day the body carries on an estimated 2 million of these biochemical reactions!

Deficiencies of vitamins & minerals over time lower the number of our body's valuable enzymes. Similarly, deficiencies of key mineral nutrients in soil which, in turn, cannot be drawn up by a plant, may lead to enzyme lowering in our body. It is critical to see, therefore, that there is a vital nutritional connection between mineral-rich soil, nutrient-rich plants, and bodily health! We literally are what we eat. And growing our own food gives us more control over its nutritional quality and our health.

From Soil . . . to Plant . . . to Person

Soil Needs
Organic matter
Sunlight
Moisture & Air
Trace minerals
Macronutrients
Microlife

Plant Needs
Soil & Minerals
Natural fertilizers
Moisture
Sunlight (for photosynthesis)
Carbon, Hydrogen, Oxygen
Insects

Human Needs
Oxygen & Water
Vitamins & Minerals
Proteins (including amino acids, enzymes, & hormones)
Carbohydrates (including fiber, sugars, & starches)
Fats (including essential fatty acids)
Love!

31

NUTRITIONAL INFORMATION *	PLANT
Serving size: 5 spears (3.5 oz) Calories: 18 Vit. A: 10% RDA Vit. C: 10 % RDA Fiber: 2 grams Protein: 2 g	**Asparagus**
Serving size: 1 medium stalk (5.5 oz) Calories: 40 Vit. A: 50% RDA Vit. C: 240% RDA Fiber: 5 grams Protein: 5 g Calcium: 6% RDA Iron: 2% RDA	**Broccoli**
Serving size: 3/4 cup (3 oz) Calories: 14 Vit. A: 2% RDA Vit. C: 8% RDA Fiber: 3 grams Protein: 1 g Calcium: 4% RDA	**Bean** (green)
Serving size: 4 oz Calories: 37 Vit. A: 110% RDA Vit. C: 33% RDA Fiber: 1 gram Protein: 1 g	**Beet**
Serving size: 1/12 medium head (3 oz) Calories: 18 Vit. A: minimal Vit. C: 70 % RDA Fiber: 2 grams Protein: 1 g Calcium: 4% RDA	**Cabbage**
Serving size: medium 7" long (3 oz) Calories: 40 Vit. A: 300% RDA Vit. C: 8% RDA Fiber: 1 gram Protein: 1 g Calcium: 2% RDA	**Carrots**
Serving size: 1/6 medium head (3 oz) Calories: 18 Vit. A: minimal Vit. C: 110% RDA Fiber: 2 grams Protein: 2 g Calcium: 2% RDA Iron: 2% RDA	**Cauliflower**
Serving size: 2 medium stalks (4 oz) Calories: 20 Vit. A: minimal Vit. C: 15% RDA Fiber: 2 grams Protein: 1 g Calcium: 4% RDA	**Celery**
Serving size: 1/2 cup cooked Calories: 20 Vit. A: 300% RDA Vit. C: 200% RDA Fiber: 2 grams Protein: 2 g Calcium: 13% RDA	**Collards**
Serving size: 1 medium ear (3 oz) Calories: 75 Vit. A: 5% RDA Vit. C: 10% RDA Fiber: 1 gram Protein: 3 g Iron: 3% RDA	**Corn**

***Note: Sources from USDA & other nutritional publications. Percent Daily Value based on 2,000 calorie daily diet. As a rule, fresh picked items have highest values**

BEST TIME TO HARVEST

STORAGE & EATING TIPS

When shoots are 6-12" high before tips open up. Upper tender part will easily snap off of lower stalk. Green spears most nutritious

Refrigerate. Wrap in damp cloth and eat within one week. Good in soups, raw in salads, or lightly steamed on low heat with tips up to preserve vitamins

Cut head when tight & fully formed but before flowering. Side shoots will develop after first cutting which may continue to be harvested before they flower

Refrigerate. Eat as soon as possible and never allow heads to yellow. Best eaten with proteins, raw or steamed on low heat

Snap variety: choose bright, fresh, tender young pods with immature seeds. They should snap easily. Keep vines picked for better production
Shell variety: let dry on bush & shell for winter.

Refrigerate. Eat while still crisp. Over-cooking destroys food value

Store in tightly sealed container in cool place. Depending on variety, use in soups, salads, dips, alone, etc.

Harvest nutrient-rich greens repeatedly at any size (roots will be smaller) or eat whole plant. Beets left in ground too long become tough

Refrigerate or Root Cellar: roots only **Overwinter** in ground in temperate climates. Steam roots & greens or grate in salads

When heads are good sized & compact. Don't let leaves become wilted-looking

Refrigerate. Use/eat as soon after cutting as possible as air exposure kills vitamin C. Eat raw in salad or lightly steam on low heat in stainless steel pan with tight lid to retain minerals & minimize gas-formation

Can be eaten at any stage, but for highest nutrient content pull at full maturity but before they get tough and skin cracks

Refrigerate, RootCellar, or Overwinter in ground. Carrots keep very well but seem to retain their crunch & vitality best in a sealed container or plastic bag in the refrigerator. Don't let them get limp. Raw carrots or juice are best. Steam until slightly firm, not soft

Best when head is creamy white, firm, heavy, & compact with outer leaves still fresh & green. When overripe head has a granular or speckled appearance and begins to separate

Refrigerate or Overwinter in ground. Can last a week or two but limpness & brown spots are a sign of decline. Great raw in salads, with dips, or in soup. Steam for a few minutes, but don't let get soft

Best celery is of medium length, density & thickness; stalks should snap easily. Pithy or stringy celery probably has lower vitamin & mineral content, and once the seed stem is forming, tastes bitter

Refrigerate or Overwinter in ground. Highly perishable. Best raw in salad and with other vegetables. Quickly steam in pan with tight lid. A good balance to foods heavy in starches or high in protein. Raw celery leaves are mineral rich

When leaves are young or full and intense color of green

Refrigerate. Use promptly either lightly steamed in soups or stir frys, or raw in salads. Good blended for baby food or special diets

When husks are fresh & green but silks have browned. Pull back husks and check for well-filled & tight-kerneled cob. Kernals should be plump & juicy, filled with thick white liquid. Test by penetrating a kernal with fingernail

Refrigerate. Steam husked ears in minimal water or cut corn kernels from ear. The sooner eaten the sweeter. Avoid yellowed husks (old or damaged), for the kernels will be tough and starchy-tasting

33

Serving size: 1/3 medium (3 oz)   Calories: 18
Vit. A: 4% RDA   Vit. C: 6% RDA
Fiber: minimal   Protein: 1 gram
Calcium: 2% RDA   Iron: 2% RDA

Cucumber

Serving size: 1/2 cup (4 oz)   Calories: 50
Vit. A: 300% RDA   Vit. C: 70% RDA
Fiber: 2 grams   Protein: 3 g
Calcium: 20% RDA   Iron: 20% RDA

Dandelions
(greens)

Serving size: 1/2 cup cooked or 1 cup raw   Calories: 20
Vit. A: 60% RDA   Vit. C: 15% RDA
Fiber: 2 grams   Protein: 2 g (Calcium: 8% RDA)

**Endive
Escarole**

Included in this chart for its rich medicinal history and for its
value as a culinary herb used often in small quantities.
For each 4 oz used, can provide 25% RDA for Vit. C

Garlic

Serving size: 1/2 cup (4 oz)   Calories: 29
Vit. A: 100% RDA   Vit. C: 140% RDA
Fiber: 2 grams   Protein: 2.75 g
Calcium: 20% RDA   Iron: 10% RDA

Kale

Serving size: 1/2 cup (4 oz)   Calories: 18
Vit. A: minimal   Vit. C: 60% RDA
Fiber: 1 gram   Protein: 1 g
Calcium: 2% RDA

Kohlrabi

Serving size: 4 oz   Calories: 50
Vit. A: minimal   Vit. C: 30% RDA
Fiber: na   Protein: 2.5 grams
Calcium: 4% RDA

Leek

Serving size: 1 cup raw   Calories: 10
Vit. A: 20% RDA   Vit. C: 4% RDA
Fiber: 1 gram   Protein: 1 g
Calcium: 4% RDA

Lettuce

Serving size: 4 oz, raw   Calories: 25
Vit. A: 100 % RDA   Vit. C: 120% RDA
Fiber: 1 gram   Protein: 2.5 g
Calcium: 15% RDA   Iron: 15% RDA

**Mustard
greens**

Serving size: 1 medium   Calories: 60
Vit. A: na   Vit. C: 20% RDA
Fiber: 3 grams   Protein: 1 g
Calcium: 4% RDA

Onion

Serving size: 4 oz, raw   Calories: 50
Vit. A: 15% RDA   Vit. C: 300% RDA
Fiber: 1 gram   Protein: 4 g
Calcium: 20% RDA   Iron: 40% RDA

Parsley

Serving size: 4 oz   Calories: 50
Vit. A: 10% RDA   Vit. C: 20% RDA
Fiber: 1 gram   Protein: 3.5 g

Pea

BEST TIME TO HARVEST	STORAGE & EATING TIPS
When firm, fresh, well-shaped, and of good medium or dark green color. Flesh should be firm, seeds small & immature. When overmature, becomes yellow, dull, shrivelled	**Refrigerate.** Eat raw in salads, or with dips, or sliced in yogurt & lemon juice. Can be juiced after removing skin for a cooling effect
Sweetest in spring when leaves are young & tender (before flowering), but can be used year-round. Avoid picking from areas or lawns sprayed with pesticides.	**Refrigerate.** Eat immediately! Best raw in salads or steamed like spinach. Dandelions are critical to natural floral habitat and especially attract honey-producing bees
The leaves may be harvested at any stage	**Refrigerate.** Best eaten raw in salads
Cut seed head as it starts to form on top of long stalk. Then dig or carefully pull up bulbs when plants begin to yellow. Dry bulbs in warm area out of sunlight	Store in dark, dry, slightly warm place. Chop fine in soups, stir frys, sauces, almost anything! Garlic's uses are almost unlimited
Start harvesting outer leaves when plant is half grown. More leaves continue to develop. Winter hardy in many climates. Avoid wilted or yellow leaves	**Refrigerate.** Cook fast & hot only a couple of minutes (overcooking destroys texture & flavor). Use in soups, stir frys, or raw in salad. Good in or with potatoe dishes
The condition of the tops is a good indicator of quality. Tops should be young & green. The thickened stem should be crisp & firm and not over 3-inches in diameter	**Refrigerate or Root Cellar.** Keeps well. Bake or steam the root. The swollen root tastes similar to a turnip only more delicate
Best harvested when stems are between 1/2 and 1 1/2 inches in diameter. Overwinters well in milder climates	**Refrigerate or Overwinter** in ground. Keeps well, but don't let get limp. Best used in soups, broths, stir frys, & some juice combinations. Excellent replacement for onion because is milder
Can be harvested at any stage by selecting leaves. The darker outer leaves are much more nutrient-rich than the pale inner leaves. Continue harvesting as leaves grow	**Refrigerate.** Keep in sealed container lined with paper towel for best storage freshness. Don't cook! Think salad!
Leaves can be picked at any size	**Refrigerate or Overwinter** in ground. Best raw in salads or slightly cooked with other vegetables. Spicy but worth developing a taste for because of high nutrient value
Pull bulbs up when long tops have fallen over. Cure in warm area out of sun until neck is dry and skin is papery	**Root Cellar or Overwinter** in ground. Keep well in burlap bag, stored in cool & fairly dry place. Lose vitamin C if overcooked. Good in everything from soups, stir frys, casseroles, to salads, sandwiches, etc.
Leaves can be picked at any stage but become more bitter once stem begins to elongate prior to flowering. Avoid yellow or limp leaves	**Refrigerate or Overwinter** in ground. Stores well. Use in every salad, in soups & casseroles, juices, and as an edible garnish
Peas are best picked when young, sweet, fresh, and tender as their food value & flavor is highest then. The pods should be bright green & well filled out, with peas that are well-developed but not bulging. Refrigerate at 32° as soon as possible	**Refrigerate.** Eat raw or steamed in pan with minimal water & tight lid soon after picking. Salt in water destroys greenness, food value & digestibility. Best eaten in combination with non-starchy vegetables to get full value of vitamin A

35

NUTRITIONAL INFORMATION   PLANT

Serving size: 1 medium   Calories: 25   **Pepper**
Vit. A: 12% RDA   Vit. C: 200% RDA   (green)
Fiber: 2 grams   Protein: 1 g

Serving size: 1 medium   Calories: 110   **Potato**
Vit. A: minimal   Vit. C: 50% RDA
Fiber: 3 grams   Protein: 3 g
     Iron: 8% RDA

Serving size: 4 oz   Calories: 20   **Pumpkin**
Vit. A: 25% RDA   Vit. C: 10% RDA
Fiber: 1 gram   Protein: 1 g

Serving size: 7 radishes   Calories: 20   **Radish**
Vit. C at 30% RDA is most nutritional quality

Serving size: 4 oz (1/2 cup cooked) Calories: 20   **Spinach**
Vit. A: 130% RDA   Vit. C: 70% RDA
Fiber: 2 grams   Protein: 2.5 g
Calcium: 10% RDA   Iron: 20% RDA

Serving size: 1/2 medium (4 oz) Calories: 20 summer, 40 winter   **Squash**
Summer squash   **Winter squash**
Vit. A: 10% RDA   Vit. A: 60% RDA
Vit. C: 30% RDA   Vit. C: 12% RDA
Protein: 1 gram   Protein: 1 g
Calcium: 3% RDA   Calcium: minimal

Serving size: 4 oz   Calories: 20   **Swiss Chard**
Vit. A: 50% RDA   Vit. C: 60% RDa
Fiber: 2 grams   Protein: 1 g
     Iron: 15% RDA

Serving size: 1 medium (4 oz)   Calories: 25   **Tomato**
Vit. A: 20% RDA   Vit. C: 40% RDA
Fiber: 1 gram   Protein: 1 g
     Iron: 2-4% RDA

Serving size: 1 medium   Calories: 80   **Apples**
Vit. C: 6% RDA
Fiber: 5 grams

Serving size: 1 1/2 cups   Calories: 85   **Grapes**
Vit. A: 3% RDA   Vit. C: 9% RDA
Fiber: 2 grams   Protein: 1 g
Calcium: 2% RDA   Iron: 2% RDA

Serving size: 1/4 - 1/10 depending on melon   Calories: 50   **Melon**
Vit. A: 10-80% RDA   Vit. C: 25-40% RDA
Fiber: 1 gram   Protein: 1 g

BEST TIME TO HARVEST	STORAGE & EATING TIPS
Harvest sweet peppers when green & plump or, even better, allow them to turn red or orange on the stalk for a huge increase in Vitamin C and amazing sweetness	**Refrigerate.** Best eaten raw to maximize vitamin C content. Chop into salads, stuff slightly baked, or slice and eat with a dip. Often used as a pizza topping as well
Numerous varieties are harvested when majority of tops have withered. Can dig early potatoes from flowering time on but it can disrupt the plant and slow future growth. Storage potatoes should be fully mature	**Root Cellar** or cool dry place out of light. Keep very well. Lose nutrients as they soften or sprout. Best eaten as raw as possible & unpeeled, or steam but don't overcook. To bake, use low heat, then 400° for the last 5 minutes only
A ripe pumpkin will be heavy for its size, with a good bright orange color and a hard rind that is difficult to scratch	Cure warm & dry out of the sun and store best at 50° at moderate humidity. Best baked or steamed. Eat plain, pie filling, etc.
Pull bulbous root when diameter is 1-11/2 inches before they get tough or crack and stalk gets long or flowers	**Refrigerate.** Eat raw in salads or with dips
Leaves may be picked at any stage and will promote new plant growth for continued harvest until plant "bolts" and flowers	**Refrigerate.** Store like lettuce. Eat raw in salad or barely cooked in tight-lidded pan or steamer without water besides that on rinsed leaves
Ripe *Summer squash* should be fairly heavy for its size and with a tender rind that can be easily scratched. *Winter squash* should have a hard rind	**Refrigerate** *Summer squash. Winter squash* stores best in root cellar like pumpkin. Best when steamed or baked, alone or in soups. Summer squash, like zucchini, is excellent raw, chopped into salads, or used in stir frys
Leaves can be cut at any stage and will promote new plant growth for continued harvest until plant "bolts" and flowers. Produces well for a year or more	**Refrigerate or Overwinter** in ground Keeps well at low temperatures. Eat raw in salads or briefly steam/stir fry with other vegetables. Overcooking destroys nutrients
Should be vine ripened & picked when fully red (or yellow or orange with some varieties). The acids in green tomatoes are hard on the body, especially the kidneys	**Refrigerate.** Best eaten fresh as in salads, or juiced in combination with other raw vegetable juices. If canned, pureed tomatoes are more nutritious than water packed. Eat combined with proteins
Apples, of course, are tree-ripened and picked when plump & full-colored for their particular variety. Most apples keep well on the tree until frost	**Refrigerate or Root Cellar** (stored alone and cold near 32°F). Best eaten raw: plain or in salads or juiced. If cooked, use low heat in stainless steel pan to preserve more of pectin, vitamins & minerals
Ready when clumps of grapes are plump & firm, yet not hard, and the color is fully developed. Ripen in fall and are often sweeter after first frost	**Refrigerate.** Eat alone or drink unsweetened juice
Generally selected by the color & firmness of rind and their sweet fragrance, depending on variety. A ripe watermelon, for example, has a dull, hollow sound when thumped, and the skin scrapes off easily	**Refrigerate** or eat fresh off vine. Keeps well when refrigerated. Best eaten alone

37

NUTRITIONAL INFORMATION   PLANT

Serving size: 1 medium   Calories: 50   **Orange**
Vit. C: 120% RDA   (including lemon
Fiber: 6 grams   Protein: 1 g   & grapefruit)
Calcium: 4% RDA

Serving size: 2 medium (6 oz)   Calories: 70   **Peach**
Vit. A: 20% RDA   Vit. C: 20% RDA
Fiber: 1 gram   Protein: 1 g

Serving size: 1 medium (6 oz)   Calories: 100   **Pear**
Vit. C: 10% RDA
Fiber: 4 grams   Protein: 1 g
Calcium: 2% RDA   Iron: 2% RDA

Serving size: 2 medium (4 oz)   Calories: 70   **Plum**
Vit. A: 10% RDA   Vit. C: 20% RDA   (& Prune)
Fiber: 1 gram   Protein: 1 g

Serving size: 4 oz   Calories: 75   **Raspberry**
Vit. C: 35% RDA
Fiber: 3 grams   Protein: 1 g
Calcium: 2% RDA   Iron: 2% RDA

Serving size: 8 medium (5.5 oz)   Calories: 50   **Strawberry**
Vit. C: 140% RDA   Fiber: 3 grams   Protein: 1 g
Calcium: 2% RDA   Iron: 2% RDA

Vitamins & Minerals	U.S. RDA	Good Garden Sources (Fruits, Vegetables & other)
A	5,000 IU	Dark leafy green vegetables, deep yellow vegies such as squashes, sweet potatoes, carrots, apricots
B complex (B_1, B_2, B_6) & folic acid	2-6 mg	Dry beans & peas (legumes), leafy greens such as spinach, lettuce, broccoli, nuts & seeds
C	60 mg	Citrus fruits & juices, strawberries, cantaloupe, tomatoes, broccoli, green vegetables, potatoes
E	30 IU	Green vegetables, legumes
K	70-140 mg	Kale, lettuce, spinach, cabbage
Calcium	1000-1500 mg	Turnip & mustard greens, collards, broccoli, dried beans & peas, spinach, chard, rhubarb
Iron	18 mg	Green leafy vegetablies, dried fruits, beans & peas
Phosphorus	1000 mg	Dried beans & peas, small amounts in most vegies
Magnesium	400 mg	Legumes, leafy green vegetables
Copper	2-3 mg	Dried beans
Potassium	1800-5600 mg	Orange juice, bananas, all vegetables

BEST TIME TO HARVEST	STORAGE & EATING TIPS
Best tree-ripened for maximum nutrition	**Refrigerate** (room temperature okay for short periods). Best to eat citrus fruit in sections, as opposed to juice, to access pulp. Pulp contains Bioflavonoids which help neutralize citric acid & retain calcium
When a peach is picked green or immature, it usually doesn't ripen well and may develop a pale, weak color, a shrivelled look, tough rubbery texture, & poor flavor. Pick when you see a red color or blush, depending on variety	**Refrigerate.** Best eaten fresh. Avoid sulfered dried peaches and those canned in heavy syrup. Think fruit salad! Or, dry in your own food dehydrator for a winter treat or a snack for home, school, work, or outdoor activity
The ripeness of a pear can be hard to determine, but watch carefully and once they start to fall from the tree, pick the rest & stack in boxes between layers of newspaper to ripen (usually a month or more). Test periodically so they don't get too soft and spoil	**Refrigerate.** Best eaten fresh or home-dried for a good winter energy food. Good in fruit salad and as cereal topping
Mature plums are plump & full-colored for the particular variety. They are also soft enough at the tip to yield to slight pressure	**Refrigerate** or dry. Plums are good eaten alone or in a fruit salad. Dried prunes, however, are the most nutritious
Mature raspberries will be plump, full-clored, and will easily separate from stem caps. Berries with attached caps may be immature & tart, while overripe ones will appear dull, soft, & excessively watery	**Refrigerate** and use within a couple days. Does not keep well and will begin to break down and mold. Good raw, in fruit salads, as a cereal topping, in pies & muffins without use of sugar
Allow to vine-ripen and pick when color is solid red and caps are still attached	**Refrigerate.** Best eaten raw or juiced without sugar. Excellent as a topping, dessert, or in fruit salad

General Functions of Vitamins & Minerals in Garden Sources

Healthy skin, good vision, strong teeth & bones, resistance to infection

Helps body use protein, fat & carbohydrates to produce energy; needed for healthy nervous system, skin, eyes, red blood cells & many other functions, including antiviral

Builds body cells, helps in healing wounds or broken bones; helps body use iron and resist infection; builds healthy teeth, gums, and blood vessels

Healthy cell membranes; preserves vitamins A & C in body
Normal blood clotting

Builds strong bones & teeth, aids in blood clotting, nerves, muscles & heart

Formation of hemoglobin which carries oxygen to the cells

Strong bones & teeth, body cells, muscle function, energy release from protein, fat & carbohydrates
Bones & teeth, muscle contraction, activiates enzymes for energy metabolism
Formation of red blood cells
Body fluid balance, muscle contraction, transmission of nerve impulses

39

The Nutrition Connection
The Protein Boost

Protein (as well as carbohydrates & fat) is needed for your body to use as energy (measured as calories). Daily protein requirements are calculated as a percentage of total calories consumed each day. This recommended percentage range is 5-8%. Check out the protein wallop of your garden in the chart below! It depicts percentage of protein *per calorie* for each item. You can find the calories per serving for various fruits and vegetables in the Nutrition Charts, pp. 32-39.

Percent of Protein Per Calorie

Vegetables		Fruits	
Spinach	49%	Lemon	16%
Broccoli	47%	Cantaloupe	9%
Cauliflower	40%	Orange	8%
Mushrooms	38%	Grape	8%
Parsley	34%	Peach	6%
Lettuce	34%	Pear	5%
Green peas	30%	Banana	5%
Zucchini	28%		
Green beans	26%	**Nuts & Seeds**	
Cucumbers	24%	Peanuts	18%
Celery	21%	Sunflower	17%
Tomatoes	18%	Walnuts	13%
Onions	16%	Almonds	12%
Potatoes	11%		

Legumes		Grains	
Soy beans	43%	Rye	20%
Lentils	29%	Wheat	17%
Split peas	28%	Oatmeal	16%
Kidney bean	26%	Buckwheat	15%
Navy bean	26%	Barley	11%
Chickpeas	23%	Brown Rice	8%

IMPORTANT NUTRITION TIP

All vegetables containing protein are lacking in one or more of the essential amino acids the body needs.

The missing amino acids can be provided by accompanying the vegetables with seeds, nuts, grains, dairy or meat (including substitutes).

Starch & Fiber:
Healthy Weight Control

Foods rich in complex carbohydrates (starches)
Your garden is a ready made weight control clinic: vegetables and fruits contain 1/2 the number of calories per ounce of fats, and more nutrients than simple carbohydrates, such as sugars.

Need More Fiber?
Fiber content of plants aid in digestion, stimulating enzyme activity in the stomach & intestines. This roughage also aids in stool development. • **Plant lots of greens, carrots, celery, and berries with edible seeds (raspberry & strawberry). Additionally, plant fruit trees.**

Need More vit. B for Energy?
The B vitamins help body cells use food energy, critical to any diet & exercise plan. **Plant more beans, peas, or dark greens like spinach & romaine lettuce.**

The High Nutrition Sampler Garden

- 2 4x12 ft raised beds (approx. 100 sq ft)
- 1-3 person family
- Intensive planting
- Companion planting

Early Spring (Plant 1st Garden Bed for late Spring early Summer harvest))

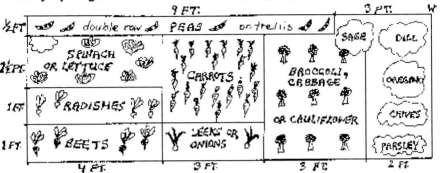

Vegetables
(high in Vitamins A & C, Calcium, Iron, fiber)
Spinach, lettuce, carrots, radishes, beets, onions (or leeks), broccoli (and/or cabbage, cauliflower), sweet peas (trellised)

Herbs
(for culinary use and for insect pest control)
Sage, dill, oregano, chives, parsley, rosemary. ***Note: Perennial herbs can be aggressive, so keep well-controlled.***

Late Spring - Early Summer
(Plant 2nd Garden Bed for late Summer and Fall harvest)

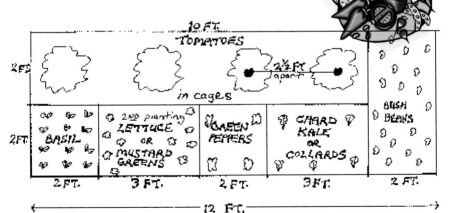

Vegetables
Tomatoes, green peppers (or red, hot, chili), chard (or kale, collards), lettuce (or other greens), bush beans, basil, nasturtiums

Herbs
Basil (great for flavoring, Italian cooking, making pesto - yummm!)

41

The Nutrition Connection
Calcium in the Garden

A home garden can add a calcium boost to one's diet. Calcium is essential for strong bones & teeth, normal blood clotting, and healthy nerves, muscles & heart. However, to use calcium the body needs an ongoing source of protein and vitamins A & D.

The U.S. RDA suggested daily calcium intake:
Adults & children 4+ years: 800-1200mg (up to 2000mg)
Adults 50+ years including pregnant, lactating or menopausal/postmenopausal women: 1000-1500mg
Teens: 1200-1800mg

A Bounty of Calcium

200 mg (1 cup chopped raw)
collard, beet & dandelion greens

150 mg (4 oz)
tofu (made from soybeans)

100 mg (1 cup chopped raw)
kale, bok choy, parsley, turnip greens

50 mg
acorn squash, baked (1/2 cup)
broccoli, raw chopped (1 cup)
orange (1 cup) or 2 figs

All of above contain usable calcium (estimated milligrams are an average of numerous studies)
NOTE: *The calcium in spinach, rhubarb, & swiss chard is largely unusable by your body because of the presence of oxalic acid in them.*

Calcium R$_x$ for Menopausal Women

Calcium is of concern for women going through life changes. Many doctors agree that principal contributors to osteoporosis are *excess proteins* — which leach calcium from the bones — and a sedentary lifestyle with a lack of weight-bearing exercise.

A low-fat, mostly vegetarian diet is high in fiber, low in fat, *and* has less protein ingestion. It provides calcium in the form of green vegetables, beans, peas, lentils, and fortified orange juice. And don't forget to add daily exercise!

What is 1 Serving?

1/2 cup cooked/chopped raw veggies
1 cup raw leafy vegies & salad
1 medium potato or tomato
1/3-1/2 cup nuts or seeds
1 cup cooked dry beans
1 green or red pepper
1 medium whole fruit
1/2 cup dried fruit
3/4 cup raw juice
1/4 small melon
1/2 grapefruit

Iron in Your Garden

Did you know that these foods, calorie for calorie, have more iron than a lean steak? — *kale, broccoli, beans, cauliflower, spinach, parsley, butterhead & looseleaf lettuce, peas, cabbage, & mustard, beet & collard greens.* Eat iron-rich foods *with* vit. C foods for absorption of "non-heme" (vegetarian) iron.

13 Most Nutritious Vegetables

Curious about what vegetables are the most nutritious? The chart below should encourage you to plant some of the 13 vegetables listed and include them in your diet. *The Golden Rule: The fresher and more naturally grown your produce, the more nutritious it will be!*

Nutrients in 1lb of Fresh Vegetables

Vegetable	Calories	Protein grams	Fat grams	Vit. A Int'l Units	Vit. C mg
Beet greens	61	6	1	15,490	76
Broccoli	89	10	1	6,920	313
Brussel Sprouts	188	21	2	2,300	426
Carrots	112	3	1	29,440	21
Chard	104	10	1	27,120	132
Kale	128	14	3	29,880	420
Mustard greens	98	10	2	22,220	308
Parsley	200	16	3	38,560	780
Bell peppers	82	5	1	1,540	476
Spinach	85	11	1	26,450	167
Squash, winter	161	5	5	11,920	43
Tomatoes	100	5	5	4,080	118
Turnip greens	127	14	2	34,470	-

NOTES

1. All dark green leafy veggies are very nutritious.

2. Iceberg lettuce is the least nutritious of greens

3. Winter squash has 6x the Vit. A as Summer squash

4. Some vegetables have good amounts of protein

5. Creatively use these veggies in your recipes

6. Homegrown veggies are incredibly fresh & tasty. Store-purchased varieties may be 1-2 weeks old and sprayed with preservatives to sustain "freshness."

Garden Sanitation

Garden sanitation is important to create overall order & control — to verify that someone is actually looking over the garden! As the tips below demonstrate, regular stewardship will insure that both your garden and harvest will be nutritious and beautiful.

Compost. Try to compost debris such as dead plants, spent flowers, grass clippings, food scraps, stalks and small twigs.

Prune. Selectively prune vegetation to enhance the beauty or feeling of a garden sanctuary.

Remove diseased plants. Funguses, diseases and certain insect infestations can significantly affect the well-being of both soil and nearby plants. Don't compost such plants, unless you can create a hot compost pile (above 150F). Best to put in garbage.

Leave something for wildlife. Plants that have gone to seed, stalks, and perhaps a small pile of twigs & branches — these provide important food & shelter for birds and other small wildlife.

General cleanliness. Clean water bowls, coil up garden hoses, put tools away, pick up debris, etc. — tidiness adds to a sense of order

Plant a Seed of Hope • Respect the Earth • Harvest Your Good Efforts

WEEDING

Weeds (unwanted plants) are the biggest killer of garden morale. We all know what to expect if we don't visit our garden for a while! Here are a few pointers:

Annuals (Miners lettuce, Foreget-me-nots, , etc.) are easily pulled or hoed when the soil is moist.

Perennials (grasses, bindweed, sedges, dandelions, etc) repeatedly resprout if cut at the surface. Pull when soil is moist.

Mulching & Intensive Planting reduce weeds by up to 2/3 because they are deprived of light and the soil is not disturbed. It is difficult for them to grow through the mulch, or they are crowded out by the canopy of plants growing close together.

Raised Beds have excellent aerated tilth that weeds can't get a good foothold in. Thus, they are easier to pull.

BE EARTH-FRIENDLY — Don't use herbicides to control weeds. They can harm soil microlife, insects, wildlife, pets, humans and even precious produce & other vegetation.

WATERING

Water is perhaps a gardener's most precious resource. It should always be treasured, conserved, and used wisely. The key is to irrigate at the proper time and in the proper amount. Most gardens need irrigating 2-3 times weekly.

Wilted plants
Plants looking wilted in early morning are already damaged from water-stress. Afternoon wilting is a warning sign to water soon.

Best time to water
Early morning or late afternoon, allowing 2 hours for the sun to dry plant leaves.

Water deeply
Whether using a sprinkler or drip irrigation, water at least 18-inches deep, especially around the outer dripline of the plant.

Weather extremes
During Summer & hot, dry, windy periods, you may need to irrigate perhaps 3 or more times weekly.

Overhead sprinkler
Set out a short can. About 1.5 inches of water collected in the can indicates soil moisture to a depth of 18 inches or more.

Exposed soil
Dense planting, cover crops, protective mulches or garden fabrics all help to retain soil moisture. Large spaces of bare soil around plants can be harmful to both soil and vegetation. It also wastes water.

Drip irrigation
Especially effective in water conservation, this method provides optimal saturation of soil deep beneath a plant's root structure. Garden centers have simple soaker hoses or complex systems, usually installed at ground level and/or beneath mulch.

SOIL TYPES

Soils are comprised of three types of rock particles (sand, silt, & clay) that vary greatly in size & shape. Sand is coarse, silt has medium-sized particles, and clay is very fine.

The Hand Test

To understand you own general soil type, rub it between your thumb and fingers or in your palm.

- **Sand** particles are gritty, whether wet or dry, and will not clump well if squeezed
- **Silt** is flour-like when dry and slightly plastic-like when moist
- **Clay** material is harsh/hard when dry and very sticky and plastic when wet. It will stick to and clog garden tools

Loam is soil which is composed of a friable (crumbly) mix of sand, silt, clay **and** organic decomposed matter. Most of the soil in the United States is a variation of loam.

Your Extension Service, local garden center or neighboring gardener can help you identify your soil type, if necessary.

Rich LOAMY SOIL is the BEST!

You probably have some combination of soil types. If you regularly add organic matter like compost, leaf mulch, tilled under cover crops, etc., you will "grow" soil that is rich in tilth and is dark & loamy

Loam
Texture: crumbly (friable)
Make-up: mixture of sand, silt, clay & decomposed organic matter; great aeration
Drainage: soil retains moisture well, therefore needs average irrigation

Clay
Texture: wet: sticky; dry: cement-like
Make-up: very fine soil particles; low aeration
Drainage: drains & dries slowly; work when crumbly and somewhat dry to best avoid creating clods

Sandy
Texture: usually loose & crumbly
Make-up: irregularly-shaped mineral particles; good aeration
Drainage: Low water-holding capacity, therefore needs very regular irrigation

Soil pH

Soil can eitheir be more acidic or more alkaline. Properly testing and balancing soil every few years optimizes plant growth. (A local Cooperative Extension Service can test it, or you can purchase a test kit like the Helige-Truog soil pH kit by Nasco).

What is pH?

pH is the acidity or alkalinity of a substance, on a scale that runs from 0-14 (7.0 = neutral, below 7.0 = acidic, above 7.0 = alkaline).

Most vegies & flowers prefer slightly acidic soil (6.0-6.8). A range from 5.0-7.0 is tolerable. Potatoes, berries, and many flowering bulbs prefer more acidic soil, ranging from 5.5-6.0.

Raising pH in Soil

Most soils are slightly acidic and need balancing about every 2-3 years. *Best time to apply: Fall*

Step 1: Add Ground Limestone

- Helps eliminate excess concentrations of substances like aluminum & manganese that can be toxic to plants
- Enhances microbial activity in the soil
- Promotes the uptake of nutrients from the soil into the plant.

Sandy soil: Use 5 lbs of lime per 100 sq ft to raise the pH one point (say from 5.5 to 6.5).
Loamy soil: Use 7.5 lbs of lime per 100 sq ft.
Clay soil: Use 10 lbs of lime (heavier soil needs more lime) per 100 sq ft to raise the pH one point.

Step 2: Add Organic Matter

Annually (In Spring or Fall) add 2-3 inches of compost (pH 6.7-7.0).

Lowering pH that is above 7.0

For Alkaline soils, especially in dry, arid regions.

Step 1: Add Organic Material

Compost is best. It contains acid-forming materials that combine with excess alkali to neutralize soil. Add 2-3 inches annually in Spring or Fall.

Step 2: Add Sulphur

Applying .5-2 lbs per 100 sq. ft can lower the pH one point. Lasts about one year.

45

COMPOSTING

A rule of thumb is to add 2-3 inches of organic matter to your soil *each year* to replace soil nutrients used up by plants *and* leached out by rain and watering. Garden compost is the ideal form of organic matter. This **Black Gold** greatly enhances your soil and its microlife. And you made it! Every gardener should compost, period! The following four pages will help you get started *(see Authors' Note below)*.

Compost: 10 Key Advantages

Earth-friendly
Lessens home kitchen and yard waste taken to a landfill by up to 35%

Increases the vitality of soil and the nutrient-richness of food plants

Replaces any need for synthetic fertilizers that may harm humans, plants, animals & micro-organisms

Improves Soil
Returns nutrients to the soil (potassium, nitrogen, phosphorous, trace minerals) all to be released slowly over 1-2 years

A natural fertilizer that improves soil aeration, tilth, & drainage

Improves population of earthworms and highly beneficial micro-organisms

Increases water retention when absorbed into loose or sandy soils; aids drainage in clay or other heavy soils

As a Mulch
Promotes weed and erosion control

Protects plant roots from sun/wind damage

Reduces soil diseases

What is Compost?

When organic matter is at an intermediate stage of decomposition, it becomes "compost." It doesn't matter if its in your compost pile or out in Nature. Compost is very dark brown and has a clean, earthy smell. Its texture is consistent (no large, undecomposed material, excepting small bits of twigs, or other particles).

Siting Your Compost Area

Easy Access. Place your pile/bin near to garden beds but out of the way

Plan for an extra bin. Many gardeners soon realize one is not enough!

Plan to stockpile materials. Holding bins help with raw or extra materials

Be neat & tidy. Organized composting is easier and is as important as a lovely garden

Water access. You will need a nearby hose and spray nozzle to moisten your pile

Compost turner. An aerator tool should be easily accessible for turning your pile

Authors' Note: Did you know our 32-page guide, ***Home Composting Made Easy***, is the most popular in the world, with over **1 million copies** in print? Go to **Resources** (page 64) for ordering details.

Plan Carefully

- **Adequate air circulation:** Create air space around bin, even if it has a cover & vents
- **Out of full sun:** This prevents excessive heat build-up in plastic bins. Partial shade is good. In any case, cover your compost pile.

- **Placement on bare ground:** For drainage of leachate, the natural liquid by-product of decomposing matter. Earthworms may also be able to migrate up into the pile when it cools down.
- **Away from large trees or shrubs:** Their roots steal nutrients from compost.
- **Away from wooden structures & fences:** They may be susceptible to rot if in contact with decomposing debris.

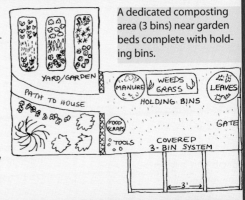

A dedicated composting area (3 bins) near garden beds complete with holding bins.

Ways to Compost

There are numerous ways to compost. Most gardeners choose to use a home-made or manufactured bin.

NOTE: Natural ways not discussed in this guide include soil incorporation, sheet composting, covered windrow, grasscycling, and vermicomposting (using worms).

Important features for a bin:

- Adequate volume (27 cubic feet is ideal) to heat pile & hold heat
- Easy to access compost
- Air vents and a lid/cover
- Scavenger resistance

Circular Collector

Made from wire or plastic, low-cost, easily assembled & moved to different locations. Best used as a holding bin when stockpiling

Tumbler

Expensive and smaller than bins. Regular rotation heats & aerates contents for fast breakdown.

Plastic Bin

Very popular. Usually small & expensive, but still gets the job done for the amount of compost produced. Available on the internet or at well stocked garden center

Home-made Bins

Commonly made from wood, pallets, cement blocks, wire, or simply a pile in the corner of the garden! Attention must be given to size, cover, scavenger resistance and air circulation.

Multi-bin System

A simple 2 or 3-bin system using available wood, pallets, & chicken wire. Front boards are removable for easy access.

Many gardeners believe that a multi-bin system is the best way to compost a lot of garden waste.

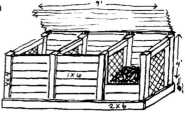

Do Compost

Carbon/Nitrogen ratios
shown in parenthesis

Green (Nitrogen)

Grass (17:1)
Weeds (20:1)
Dead vegetation (20:1)
Food scraps (15:1)
Fruit waste (40:1)
Manure (7-20:1)
Coffee grounds (20:1)
Tea bags
Hair, lint

Brown (Carbon)

Leaves (35-85:1)
Weeds/Grass (dry) (30:1)
Straw/hay (80:1)
Paper (170:1)
Compost, humus (10:1)
Wood chips* (700:1)
Sawdust* (140-700:1)
*use cautiously!

Don't Compost

Meat, grease, bones
Dairy Products
Weeds with seeds
Diseased plants
Cat, dog, human waste
Very soggy materials
Branches
Wood ashes
BBQ charcoal
Lime

Making Compost in 8 Steps

1. **Course Materials on Bottom.**
   Place shredded or chopped-up coarse materials (large weeds, stalks, etc.) on bottom for drainage & aeration.

2. **Layered or Mixed.**

   Batch Pile: Add materials in layers of about 2-3 inches, using Steps 3, 4, & 5 below as your guide.
   Add-as-you-go Pile: Add mixed variety of materials as they become available, carefully balancing Greens & Browns in suggested ratios.

3. **Green & Brown Matter.** Alternate Brown/carbon materials with Green/nitrogen materials. These can be equal parts by volume, or a ratio of 2 parts Green to 1 part Brown (best).

4. **Activator.** Dust on a small amount of "activator" in each layering cycle (or into mixed pile), if desired.

5. **Moisture.** Keep pile moist to the consistency of a damp sponge (check moisture level weekly).

6. **Seal.** Always have a layer of Brown material on top of a pile to keep flies and scavengers away from food scraps.

7. **Turn.** Every 7-10 days turn the pile (use a shovel, garden fork or aerator) to bring outer layers into the center where temperatures are the hottest. Turning heats up the pile again.
   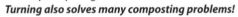
   Turning also solves many composting problems!

8. **Cover.** Keep pile or bin covered at all times, insuring adequate air flow into and around it.

What is C/N?

Compostable material is commonly identified by the ratio of two elements: Carbon (Brown) & Nitrogen (Green). The ideal mix of C/N is **30:1** (up to 50:1) for fastest decomposition. High Carbon content causes slow breakdown (little heating of pile). Green/Nitrogen is needed to heat up a pile.

Generally, mixing 2 parts **Green** to 1 part **Brown** (or equal parts at most) will give you a heated pile, if proper moisture & aeration is maintained, and material is small, well chopped up, or shredded.

A Well-Heated Pile

A good pile of optimal volume will heat up in a few days or so, hopefully rising to

a temperature of 150F or higher. This important process allows essential bacteria and other micro-organisms to consume the materials. Repeated turning of the pile (every 7-10 days) will re-heat it.

About Activators

A well-made compost pile, mixed with Greens & Browns, will heat up well to decompose matter. A Nitrogen-rich Activator can also be added as a boost.

Common Activators
(% Nitrogen-Rich)

Coffee grounds	2.1%
Rabbit manure (fresh)	2.4 %
Rabbit manure (dry)	12.0 %
Alfalfa meal	2.4 %
Bonemeal	4.0 %
Cottonseed meal	7.0 %
Chicken manure (dry)	8.0 %
Bloodmeal	15.0 %

Activators are available as powders (meals), manures (fresh or dry), enzyme-acting, or a commercially boxed blend (5lbs).

The easiest application to your compost pile is to intermix with the layers of material. Powders and blends are sprinkled in sparingly; manures a little more generously applied. Remember: A little goes a long way!

4 RULES OF COMPOSTING

Rule 1: *QUALITY MATERIALS & ACTIVATORS:* Mixed together or well-layered (with attention to balance of Greens to Browns)

Rule 2: *VOLUME:* Pile is adequate size (about 3x3x3 feet) for it to heat up and be turned

Rule 3: *MOISTURE:* Pile is kept the consistency of a damp sponge

Rule 4: *AIR CIRCULATION:* Pile/bin is vented and covered (make sure it is scavenger proof)

Stockpiling

One of the best ways to guarantee a supply of materials to compost is Stockpiling. This means storing certain Greens and Browns until you are ready to compost them.

A covered wire or wooden holding bin near your compost pile is

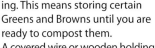
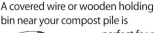

perfect for storing leaves, weeds, manure, grass clippings or other yard waste. Household food scraps can be stored in a 4-5 gallon, tightly lidded pail. Sheets of newspaper between lid & pail keep flies out. For each addition of food scraps to pail, sprinkle sawdust, soil, peat moss, or finished compost on top to control flies or odor.

TROUBLESHOOTING

Too Wet
Soggy materials & not enough air
Solution: Add dry Brown matter & turn the pile

Too Dry
Moisten without saturating pile

Pile Won't Heat Up
Too much Brown matter
Solution: Add Green/ Nitrogen matter and/or activator

Ammonia Smell
Too much Green/Nitrogen.
Solution: Add Brown matter & turn the pile

Rotten Eggs Smell
Too wet with little oxygen
Solution: Turn the pile & add Brown matter

Flies & Gnats
Uncovered food waste
Solution: Always cover exposed food waste with Brown material

Rodents , Raccoons, etc.
Possible meat & fatty food (or exposed food waste)
Solution: Remove from pile, turn; scavenger-proof bin with small mesh wire

Finished Compost Not Uniform in Texture
Chop or shred materials better; try to get pile hotter to decompose matter

Compost has Weeds
Pile didn't get hot enough to kill weed seeds; don't put "weeds-gone-to-seed" in pile

No Earthworms?
Not a problem at all!

49

COVER CROPPING: For Healthy Soil

For centuries, farmers and gardeners have restored vital health to soil through cover cropping (and composting!). Also called a *green manure*, *catch crop*, or *live mulch*, it is very inexpensive to plant, nurture, and intermix with regular crops. Plus! Some cover crops, like legumes and greens, can be eaten.

For the home gardener, we recommend planting legumes and greens as a cover crop, both for edible nutrition and exceptional restoration of much-needed nitrogen and other nutrients to the soil.

SAVE the PLANET
Cover Crops: Giving Back to the Soil

Cover crops increase the amount of organic matter in the soil, thereby stimulating its ability to hold nutrients

Cover crops loosen heavy soils allowing better air and water penetration

Cover crops prevent erosion or soil compaction due to rain, snow, wind

Cover crops (especially legumes) restore nitrogen (plus atmospheric nitrogen) and other nutrients to the soil, usable for several months

Cover crops, via their deep fibrous root systems, bring leached nutrients back to the surface for plant uptake

Cover crops can be planted in early spring through late fall, depending on your purpose

Cover crops generally require only small amounts of fertilization and a minimal amount of care

Cover crops are often edible and quite delicious (such as Austrian field peas, corn salad, tyfon, fava beans)

Types of Cover Crops

There are generally four types, with legumes and greens being easiest and best to grow in home gardens.

Legumes: Austrian field peas, clovers (red, crimson, white), fava beans, cow peas, vetches, soybeans
Greens: Corn salad, tyfon, mustard
Grains: Winter oats or wheat, rye, buckwheat, alfalfa, millet, barley
Grasses: Rye grass (annual), Sudan grass

Make a Wise Choice

1. Choose a **quick-growing** cover crop, such as a legume (especially if you plant in fall)
2. Choose a cover crop that **protects the soil and shades out weeds**
3. Choose a cover crop that is **suited to your climate and soil and is hardy enough,** if planted to overwinter, to survive your typical winter weather conditions (i.e. know the hardiness zone for your region)
4. Choose a cover crop that can be **easily turned into the soil** with a shovel or pitchfork

Cover Crop in 4 Easy Steps →

Legumes & Greens: Great Cover Crops!

Crop	When to Plant	Characteristics
Austrian field peas (1-3 ft tall)	Sept to mid-Oct or early spring	**Sow 1-2 lbs per 100 sq ft.** Leaves & purple flowers are edible & delicious; adds nitrogen to soil; somewhat cold hardy; tolerates poor soil
Cowpea	Spring after last frost	**Sow 1-2 lbs per 100 sq ft.** Very fast growing annual which thrives in all parts of U.S. in a wide variety of soils; is a fine soil builder; its massive roots can crack hardpan
Crimson clover (12-24")	Sept to Oct. (4-6 weeks before first hard frost)	**Sow 1oz per 100 sq ft.** Good for well-limed, well-drained, more fertile soils; adds nitrogen to soil and is an excellent soil builder; beautiful flowers; cold hardy; doesn't multiply with runners like red clover
Fava beans (4-6 ft tall)	Sept to Oct or early spring	**Sow 1-2 lbs per 100 sq ft.** Hardier varieties survive most winters down to 5-10F; produce 2x the nitrogen of clovers; one of the most nutritious cover crops; Rot quickly once turned under; striking appearance & unusually beautiful flowers; better varieties are edible
Red clover (1-2 ft tall)	Spring or Fall (mild climates)	**Sow 1oz per 100 sq ft.** Deep-rooted biennial produces most growth 2nd year if not allowed to seed in 1st season; adapted to wide range of soil conditions; likes organic matter & pH of 6.0 or above; one of most nutritional of cover crops; likes plenty of rain and mild winters & summers; bees love it
Vetch (2-5 ft tall)	Spring in colder climates; Fall	**Sow 2-3oz per 100 sq ft.** Annual & biennial varieties available; likes moderately fertile soil & ample moisture; hairy vetch thrives in sandy or acid soils & is most winter hardy; Hungarian variety is good for wet soils with mild winters; shade tolerant & easy to till under
Alfalfa	Spring (cold climates) Late Summer (warmer areas)	**Sow 2-3oz per 100 sq ft.** Deep-rooted perennial legume; does well in all but very clayey, sandy, acid, or poorly drained soils; add lime if pH is 6.0 or below, and colloidal or rock phosphate; attracts beneficial insects
Corn salad (12-18")	Early Sept	**Sow 1oz per 100 sq ft.** Very hardy; self-sowing in a non-invasive way; delicious salad green until bolting in April; dense roots harder to turn under; germination is sometimes tricky, so planting early in September is a must
Tyfon/Mustard	May to early Aug	**Sow 1/2oz per 100 sq ft.** Great salad green tasting like mustard; pick winter greens until bolts in March; easily hand-pulled from soil for early Spring crops; grows rapidly, cold hardy; strong tap root breaks up heavy soils

his way! 🖝

COVER CROPPING: 4 Easy Steps

STEP 1:   Choose What to Plant & When

Home gardeners best benefit by planting a cover crop that is a legume or a green. Plentiful nitrogen is restored to the soil, and parts of the plant can be eaten while it is growing. Study the chart on page 49 to make a choice.

Overwinter cover crops
Remember to plant overwintering cover crops early enough so that they have 4-6 weeks to get established before frost or cold weather slows their growth. Usually September to mid-October is the best time to sow.

Spring & Summer cover crops
Hardier Spring-sown varieties are usually planted late February through April. Summer cover crops may be planted after the last Spring frost through mid-July or so. If in doubt, be brave enough to experiment and keep records of your efforts and results.

Special Note: If your previous crop (for example, corn or tomatoes) is still in place, you can still seed your cover crop in-between the rows or around the plants. When the plants are finally expired, cut them off at ground level so that the cover crop can then fill in.

What to Buy

Seeds can be obtained inexpensively by the packet, or in bulk.

Try a good garden center, online supplier, or save your own seeds.

Natural organic complete fertilizer mixes can be purchased by the box or homemade.

STEP 2: Prepare Your Soil

First, spade or loosen up the top 8-10 inches of soil **Next,** mix organic matter and any necessary fertilizers into the top 6 inches or so.

About adding fertilizer
Have poor soil? Mixing a couple inches of compost or well-aged manure into your soil can be helpful along with a small amount of complete organic fertilizer (see **Natural Fertilizers,** pp. 14-17). The exact amount will depend on the fertility of your soil and when you last fertilized.

If you are planting a legume, you will need little or no nitrogen. However, adding **phosphorous** (such as bonemeal, colloidal phosphate or rock phosphate), **potassium** (such as kelpmeal, greensand, or rock dust), and enough **lime** to get your pH between 6.0-6.8 may be helpful. By fertilizing your cover crop, its growth will usually be better and more organic matter and nutrients will eventually be added to the soil as a result.

STEP 3
Plant Your Cover Crop

Small seeds
It is easiest to broadcast (evenly scatter) your seed over the surface of the seed bed. Small seeds need only to be covered with a light raking/sprinkling of soil.

Large seeds
Field peas, fava beans, etc. are planted to a depth of about 1.5 inches. Rake aside the soil to cover them to that depth before you broadcast, or you can poke the seeds down individually with your finger.

Firm soil well over seeds & keep moist. In marginal weather, protection with a layer or two of reemay (a lightweight garden fabric, available at well-stocked garden centers) or other "floating row cover" can speed germination.

STEP 4:   Turn It Under

Cover crops (or green manures) are cut before seed formation begins (profuse blossoms) because at that point the energy of the plant moves up from the roots into seed production and the vegetation also becomes tougher and more resistant to quick rotting.

Cut & Turn Under When Flowers Bloom

For immediate replanting:
Cutting the crop as flowering begins is usually the best time. If the growth is heavy, chop it up (use a hoe or pointed edge of a shovel) before working it into the soil, or cut down the vegetation, rake it up, compost it, and then hoe in the remaining stubble. This last method would allow immediate replanting.

A good reason to wait 2-3 weeks:
Wait 2-3 weeks for the remains of your chopped-up cover crop to decompose enough to permit easy planting. If you do not wait to plant, the decomposing raw plant material could steal soil nutrients from the new crop.

ADD FINISHED COMPOST TO CROP RESIDUE

TURNING UNDER FAVA BEANS

Voila! — A Natural Fertilizer

Whether you mow or turn under, *leave the root systems of your cover crop in the soil* (they are 50% of the weight of the plant!) — they will rot quickly and will break up the soil two feet deep or more — much deeper than a rototiller.

Legumous root systems will be covered with little white nodules which store nitrogen. Properly grown cover crops will have an N-P-K ratio of approximately 2% nitrogen, .5-.8% phosphorous, and 3-6% potassium. The amount of plant food per acre left by cover crop residue is said to equal one ton of high grade fertilizer. Cool!

MULCHING: Protecting the Soil

Bare soil is murder in a garden — hard as a rock, maybe weed-ridden, nutrients leached out by heat, wind and moisture. Mulch, however is soil's best friend. Mulching is like supplying your plants and soil with an "umbrella" of protection. It has diverse uses, so be sure to incorporate it into your gardening efforts.

SAVE the PLANET

Mulching: Key to Soil Safety

Mulching is a satisfying way to protect Earth's precious soil. When applied to the soil surface it has these benefits:

Retains moisture
A key value of mulching! Dew & evaporation can be reduced 10-50%, meaning less necessary watering.

Insulates & stabilizes the soil
Mulch keeps the soil around plant roots cooler during warm weather and warmer during cool nights and fall/winter. Mulch prevents soil compaction & crusting from rain, and controls wind & water erosion. Living mulches also stimulate earthworm and microlife activity and add organic matter back to the soil.

Protects plants, seeds & starts
Mulch cools plant roots & soil on warm days. It also inhibits soil-borne diseases from infecting plants via water splash onto leaves, flowers & fruits. Live mulches give much-needed nutrients to the soil.

Controls weeds
Deep-enough mulches can reduce weeding by as much as two-thirds. Any weeds will generally be shallow-rooted and easy to pull.

Types of Mulches

Mulches are basically organic or inorganic (also see page 54).

Organic mulches are the most natural and eventually break down into humus (dark, rich, well-decomposed organic matter), thus enriching the garden's topsoil.

Inorganic mulches, while effective, do not add nutrients to the soil. However, they do protect bare soil very well.

The most effective mulch should be 1) light and open enough to let water and air pass through, and 2) heavy enough to stay in place to inhibit weed growth.

How Much to Use

Mulches vary in density and compaction. It is always difficult to estimate how much to use. Experience is the best teacher. However, the chart below is a helpful guide.

Amount of Organic Material Needed to Cover 100 sq ft	
Depth	**You Need**
6 inches	2 cubic yds
4 in.	35 cubic ft
3 in.	1 cubic yd
2 in.	18 cubic ft
1 in.	9 cubic ft
100 sq ft = two 4x12 ft beds, 12" high	

Uses of Mulch

Vine Crops

Straw mulch keeps vine crops like squash, cucumbers & tomatoes from rotting when contacting wet soil.

Blueberries

6 inches of aged sawdust is perfect for acid- and moisture-loving blueberries, rhododendrons & azaleas.

Vegetables love a cooling mulch in the heat of Summer.

DON'T MULCH . . .

Newly seeded beds
If you don't want slugs, snails, sow bugs, etc. hiding out to eat tender plants or seeds, don't mulch!

Early Spring plantings
Soil is cold and the sun is needed to warm it up and stimulate root growth. So, don't mulch!

Overwintering crops
Those lucky enough to grow food during winter need warmth, not cooling. So, don't mulch (except for root crops.

Root Crops

A 6-8 inch mulch of shredded leaves or straw placed over root crops (potatoes, carrots, garlic, onions), once the tops die back, can allow "in the ground" storage through the winter, if possible in your area.

Fruit Trees

A nutritious living mulch of white clover or a soft mulch under fruit trees will save water, keep down weeds, and prevent falling fruit from bruising.

Paths

Bark mulch is great for paths, near hose bibs, between vegetable beds (as is a live mulch!), and general landscaping.
Other mulching options for paths or between raised/mounded beds are straw, cardboard, carpet scraps, landscape fabric, etc.

MULCHING GUIDE & TIPS

Guide to Mulches

Organic mulches are readily available, inexpensive, and enhance the soil. Inorganic mulches are not made from plant materials, are relatively expensive and add nothing to the soil. Use this guide to determine what appeals to you, is available in your area or garden, and/or might give you the benefits you desire.

Organic Mulches	Applied Thickness & Comments
Feeding Mulches (compost, leaves)	**1-3+"** Very good for moisture retention, weed control, & insulation; Supplies fertilizer & trace minerals during decomposition. Generally aesthetic.
Seed-Free Mulches (straw, hay)	**6-8"** Excellent all-round mulch. Get 2nd or 3rd cuttings to eliminate weed-seeds. Functional but not aesthetic.
Living Mulches (ground covers, herbs)	**Varies** These low-lying, shallow-rooted, ground covers return annually and look natural in the garden providing many good mulching benefits
Cover Crops (crimson clover, vetch, fava beans, Austrian field peas, ryegrass, buckwheat, etc.)	**Varies** Known as "green manures," these are seeded annually and are highly prized for giving Nitrogen to the soil. Tilled directly into the soil, they are very beneficial for overwintering in the vegetable beds.

Inorganic Mulches

Plastic	**1-6 mil** Non-moisure absorbancy means the ground must be moist before applying. May make soil too warm, yet controls weeds. Adds nothing to soil, unaesthetic.
Geotextiles	**1-2 layers** Landscape fabrics made from polypropylene or polyester. "Reemay", a gauzy fabric is popular. Provide good mulching benefits, especially in frost danger
Stone	**2-4"** Dark stone retains heat, light stone reflects heat. Mostly used in landscaping in paths, around trees & shrubs.

Special Thoughts About These Mulches . . .

Grass Clippings	**1" max** Fresh cut grass rots quickly & smells, yet adds organic matter & Nitrogen to the soil. Mats easily, so mix with other mulch materials. May carry weed seeds & herbicides.
Wood/Bark Chips	**2-3"** Good permanent mulch which decomposes slowly. Limited use in vegetable garden except between paths.
Sawdust	**1-2"** Use caustiously. Not an all-round effective mulch; decomposes slowly and ties up Nitrogen in soil, causing plants to become yellow & stunted. Is used at base of blueberries & rhododendrons, however.
Peat Moss	**1"** Best as soil conditioner, not as mulch. Absorbs too much water and adds nothing to the soil.

MULCHING TIPS

Gardening from year-to-year increases one's skill and awareness in detecting plant and soil needs. By regularly mulching, you will understand the effectiveness of different kinds of mulch; you will even develop some preferences and favorites. Additionally, certain mulching issues may arise. Here are a few to be aware of.

Nitrogen Deficiency
Q. How will Nitrogen deficiency show up in mulching?
A. Plants & crops may look yellow and stunted. Using fresh sawdust, bark mulch or woodchips may cause this as they steal nutrients from the soil. Add some extra Nitrogen to the soil before mulching with these.

Soil Types
Q. How much mulch should be applied to different soil types?
A. Apply thicker mulches to sandy, gravelly soils, which tend not to hold moisture. Apply thinner mulches to heavy clay soil which retain moisture longer. Do not mulch in low-lying places because of excessive moisture pooling in soil.

Mulching Seedlings
Q. How should seedlings be mulched?
A. Wait until the plants are 1-2" higher than the thickness of the mulch you will be applying. Also, do not pack mulch tightly around stems until plant is well established.

Vegetables love a cooling mulch in the heat of Summer

Replacing or Turning
Q. When should mulch be replaced or turned?
A. Replace mulch when it has decayed or compacted, unless it has decomposed into the soil. You can also fluff it up with a pitchfork.

Shallow Root Growth
Q. Can mulching promote shallow root growth?
A. Yes it can because the soil stays relatively moist beneath the mulch. If you start mulching, you should sustain its use during the warm season, otherwise its removal may severely stress plants by excessive heating of the bare soil.

Slugs & Snails
Q. What about slug or snail infestation due to mulching?
A. Prevention is important! Slugs & snails like moisture but nothing abrasive. Spread rock dust, or diatomaceous earth beneath mulch. Reapply if necessary.

Removing Mulch
Q. When are the best times to remove mulch?
A. After the last Spring frost, any wintered-over mulch should be removed to aid in heating up the soil. Reapply if desired when hot weather begins. Similarly, remove late Summer mulch so that the soil of any Fall crops can stay heated enough to stimulate growth before Winter mulch is applied. Most organic mulches can be composted.

BENEFICIAL INSECTS

Your garden is a natural host to many insects, good and problematic. Beneficial insects are critical to the concept of Integrated Pest Management (IPM), where key plants (flowers, herbs, vegetables, grasses) encourage good bugs to happily live & protect other plants.

The insects you want in your garden are **Pollinators** (bees, butterflies), **Predators** (direct eaters) and **Parasites** (lay eggs in prey).

10 Key Insects in Your Garden

Syrphids (hover flies) love aphids

Predacious Ground Beetle In both larval & adult stages, feeds at night on insects like cutworms, maggots, snails & slugs

Spiders (not actually in the insect family) prey on many insect pests

Minute Pirate Bug loves thrips, small aphids, spider mites, various insect eggs, & small larvae

Parasitic Wasps lay eggs in the egg, larval, or adult forms of pests, killing them

Lacewings Larvae feed on aphids, scale, small catterpillars, moth eggs, & mealybugs

Lady Beetles (ladybugs) eat many types of insects & aphids

Flies The larval stage parasitizes & kills insects; adults attach to the larvae of butterflies, moths, caterpillars, etc. laying eggs in their hosts

Where is #9 & #10?

58

SAVE the PLANET

4 Ways to Attract Beneficials to Your Garden

Step 1	**Plant Flowers, Herbs, Grains, Grasses**
Step 2	**Use a Beneficial Bug Food** (if needed)
Step 3	**Plant a Hedgerow**
Step 4	**Practice Companion Planting** (pp. 16-18)

Bug Food for Beneficials

Mmm...

To attract or maintain high levels of beneficial bugs when nectar, pollen, or prey are not very abundant, you can mix-up your own bug food!

Aphid eaters such as lacewings & ladybugs love this brew:

1 part whey or brewers yeast
1 part sugar
10 parts water (spray or spread the mixture)

Commercially-made bug foods are also available. Look for names such as "Bug Chow" and "Bug Pro," among others

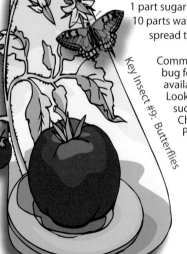

Key Insect #9: Butterflies

BUG CHOW

Plant Nectar-Rich Flowers

The importance of flowers in the garden to attract beneficial insects cannot be overstated. Here's a few reasons.

1. Many predators/parasites need **nectar & pollen** to supplement their diet of insects
2. Pollen & nectar plants are sources for **carbohydrates, amino acids & other key compounds** — survival needs for insects

3. **Few flowering plants = fewer beneficial insects**. Even purchased insects, like ladybugs, will fly away without flowers around

4. **Flowering weeds & wildflowers** attract more beneficial insects than fancy hybrid flowers
5. **Wildflowers among fruit trees** attract enough beneficial parasites to destroy up to 18X the number of munching tent caterpillars and codling moths
6. **Notice where beneficials feed**. Consider protecting these plants and/or planting more in a hedgerow on the borders of the garden

Nectar-Rich Flowers

The Carrot Family
Celery, coriander, parsnips, dill, Queen Anne's Lace

The Daisy Family
Black-eyed Susans, coreopsis, asters, goldenrod, chamomile, bachelor's buttons, yarrow, Joe-pye weed, marigolds

Others to Ponder
Milkweed, buckwheat, catnip, & crops that have flowered (like broccoli, mustard, radish, asparagus)

Plant a Hedgerow

Not everything in a garden needs to be well organized. A "wild" border is one of the very best ways to attract beneficial insects (and birds & butterflies), giving them food, thermal protection, and a good home to raise a family.

*   A hedgerow is a permanently planted strip of land left wild. It usually is at least 3-ft wide and any length
*   It can be planted around the border or fence of a garden plot. A nearby water source, like a pond, is ideal
*   It may contain a variety of grasses, clovers & wildflowers, and should include at least a few of the specific plants listed on this page
*   It creates a permanent safe habitat for a number of insects, many of who will be beneficial

PEST CONTROL

Many insects seasonally reside in a garden. They are part of a vast **Web of Life** that includes the soil, vegetation and other "wildlife", large and minute. A vast industry of products, techniques, and schools of thought reflect the gardener's desire to control Nature, especially insects.

We caution using a "military" approach toward controlling out-of-balance insect populations. Creative gardeners have found the best success by following the ten planet saving approaches below and throughout this book. Otherwise, natural botanical sprays, soaps and traps are earth-friendly, safe, and least toxic.

SAVE the PLANET

Pest Control: 10 Earth-Friendly Strategies

- Observe Without Judgment
- Use Least Toxic Methods
- Build Soil Health
- Promote Diversity
- Use Companion Planting
- Practice Cover Cropping
- Practice Crop Rotation
- Right Plant, Right Place
- Use Open-pollinated Seeds
- Experiment & Adapt

The Best Pest Control:

OBSERVE WITHOUT JUDGMENT
Be curious and attentive to varieties of insects before thinking that killing them is best

USE LEAST TOXIC METHODS
Don't use anything that can harm wildlife, plants, pets or humans beyond the specific pest or conditions used for

Least Harmful Methods

Hand Removal

Water. A strong blast can wipe out aphids and other pesky pests.
Pruners/Gloves. Remove pest-ridden leaves, stems, blooms; snip tent caterpillars.
Rake. Remove diseased leaves; don't compost.

Traps & Barriers

Sticky Traps. A sticky barrier (such as Tanglefoot) with one or more attractants (color, smell, shape) to lure the target pest in and keep it there.
Slug Traps. Common examples: trap under small wooden boards, clay pots, citrus rinds (grapefruit); a shallow container of beer attracts them too (use with other methods for best results). Remove trapped slug by hand.

Insecticidal Sprays

Made from salts of fatty acids (from animals & plants) — help control many soft-bodied insects (like aphids) when mixed with water & sprayed. Very safe. Samples:
Bio-Neem. Restricts appetite & growth
GreenBan. Repels with its smell
B.T. (bacillus thuringiensis). Paralyzes digestive system

Floating Row Cover. Drape a lightweight fabric (Reemay) over plants to ward off insects.
Copper Slug Barrier. A 3-inch wide sheet of copper prevents slugs from crossing over onto plants by giving them an electrical shock
Sticky Barrier. Prevents insects & mites from walking up trunks or stems of trees, shrubs and other plants. Trade name: Tanglefoot or Tangletrap.
Diatomaceous Earth. Its gritty texture wards off slugs. Spread around plants.
Netting. Drape garden netting (such as "strawberry netting") over fruiting plants to ward off birds.

Homemade Natural Sprays

For Aphids, White Flies & Spider Mites Mix 1Tbs biodegradable dish soap to 1 cup cooking oil to make a stock solution. Mix 1-3 tsp of stock with 1 cup water. Spray plants every 10 days

For Various Caterpillars & Beetles (repels cabbage worms, Mexican Bean beetles, Colorado potato beetles, etc.)

 Cover leaves & stems of a handful of nasturtiums with water & liquify in blender. Strain, add a bit of mild soap & spray on plants. Experiment! (Try using a catnip spray, prepared as above, for beetles & other insects as well)

All-Purpose Quick Spray (effective!) Spray to repel flea beetles, Japanese beetles, leafminers, Mexican bean beetles, potato beetles, etc. Pour on soil to protect plants from fungal diseases.

Blend 1 chopped onion, 1 clove garlic, 1/4 tsp cayenne pepper, a little water. Strain through cheesecloth and dilute with 1 quart water & 1 tsp dish soap.

Last Resort Botanical Remedies

Botanical remedies are plant-derived and, although "natural," there is a range of toxity gardeners should be aware of.

Organic growers may have "last resort" favorites. These are commonly known as Pyrethrum, Rotenone, Ryania, & Sabadilla, and come under several labels with a variety of strengths.

We do not recommend these if other options are available — their toxity requires careful handling and can harm wildlife beyond the specific pests/conditions used for.

WILDLIFE STEWARDSHIP

Be Respectful & Earth-Friendly

Your garden is a complex *Web of Life*. From microorganisms in the soil to insects, birds or even dreaded slugs, moles, gophers, raccoons, deer, etc., a multi-seasonal drama is at play. And this deserves your respect.

Perhaps the best lesson to learn in gardening is that our own impatience and fear may create the so-called pests we may see in our garden. *Therefore, get acquainted with the wildlife, large & small, in your garden.* Patiently observe, relax, be curious. Get down on ground level and withhold judgment. Do this regularly as the seasons turn. Your knowledge of the comings-and-goings of most small wildlife & insects in your garden will help you to make wiser choices about their management.

You can have a co-creative adventure with the wildlife in your garden. *Most are not pests! And dare it be said that, as gardeners, we risk being the biggest pest in our vegetable patch!*

Use Least Harmful Strategies

Design your garden (using the ideas in this book) to create a dynamic yet balanced ecosystem that will provide a year-round habitat for beneficial insects, birds and other wildlife. Always strive to use the least harmful or most humane ways to control pests — ways that don't use poisons or traps that may harm other beneficial wildlife, humans, the soil, water sources, and important vegetation.

- Plant a variety of vegetation — nectar & food-producing plants for each season (seeds & nuts, berries & soft fruits, nectar-rich herbs & flowers).
- Plant trees, shrubs, grasses & bushes for food, nesting, cover & shelter from the heat or cold.
- Provide water sources (pond, filled saucers, a barrel, marshy soil), sitting perches (trellises, stumps, logs, twigs), and even birdhouses, feeders, and a birdbath.

BIRDS & BUTTERFLIES

One of the great joys of gardening is admiring such visitors as birds and butterflies. Each has a roaming territory, and if you offer them food, water & shelter they will come.

A key strategy is to create a natural setting that has a diversity of nectar and food producing plants, either intermixed in your garden beds or planted on the borders. Here are some ideas.

Birds Love Fruit-Bearing Shrubs & Vines

Summer
Blackberry
Blueberry
Cherry
Currant
Mulberry
Raspberry
Serviceberry
Rose (hips)

Fall
Bittersweet
Crabapple
Dogwood
Huckleberry
Grapes
Cranberrybush
Juniper
Privet
Salal

Winter/Spring
Barberry
Bayberry
Cotoneaster
Holly
Mountain ash
Osoberry
Pyracantha
Russian olive

Note: You may need to protect some of your fruits from excessive munching

Provide Supplemental Bird Food

Providing supplemental food for birds, especially in winter, can greatly increase the number & species visiting your yard. Place your bird feeders in an easily observable location — for the birds and you!

White Proso Millet
Brown-headed Cowbird
Dark-eyed Junco
House (English) sparrow
Mourning Dove
Sparrows (most)
Red-Winged Blackbird

Black-Striped Sunflower
ScrubJay
Chickadees
Tufted Titmouse
Nuthatches
Brown Thrasher
Common Grackle
Pine Siskin
Some Sparrows

Oil (Black) Sunflower
Cardinal
Chickadees
Evening Grosbeak
Purple (& House) Finch
Mourning Dove

Peanut Kernals
BlueJay
Tufted Titmouse
Mourning Dove

Hulled Sunflower
American Goldfinch
Common Grackle
House Finch
White-throated Sparrow

WATER TIPS

Shallow sources. Ponds, pools, bird baths, etc. will often attract more wildlife than any other landscape feature. Most birds like very shallow water for bathing (less than 1" for songbirds!), so try to make sure that whatever water source you create has a shallow area

Bird baths. Clean and refill them regularly, even in winter

Loafing islands. For ponds, create "loafing islands" such as an exposed rock, a crook created by a partially submerged log, and the like. A host of small creatures such as frogs, lizards, newts, turtles, and water-loving birds will frequent such natural environments

Tips for Butterfly Lovers

Let them sunbathe! Butterflies cannot fly if their body temperature is too low. Sunbathing warms up their wings for flight. *Lay out some nice flat rocks here & there for them to rest on*

Give them water! Place a few shallow saucers of water on the ground, create a pond or bog, or place a "sunning rock" in a birdbath

Plant extras! Butterfly larva may only feed on the leaves of a couple of plants. So, *plant extra so there is enough for all.* Native plants (wild ones even more than cultivated) are ideal for butterfly larva!

Plant in groups! Group several of a certain type of nectar-rich plant together for easy access

The Need for Shelter

Birds (& wildlife) need *Hiding cover* (from predators), *Nesting cover,* and *Thermal cover* (from weather). These work well:

Trees, shrubs, snags, wild grasses, birdhouses, rock piles, general garden debris

Water sounds. By arranging a waterfall effect, fountain, or dripping water, you will attract attention and enjoy the pleasing sounds as well

Water-holding objects. A small ceramic bowl, a slightly hollowed-out rock, etc. attract curious visiting birds & critters

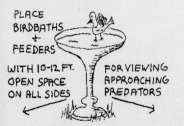

PLACE BIRDBATHS + FEEDERS

WITH 10-12 FT. OPEN SPACE ON ALL SIDES

FOR VIEWING APPROACHING PREDATORS

Nectar-Rich Food for Butterflies

Butterflies need a mix of flowering annuals, perennials & shrubs that will provide nectar and egg-laying sites for the adults. Once the eggs hatch, the larvae (caterpillars) have voracious yet selective appetites for a few weeks before entering the pupil stage. *Adult and larval food plants are your best assurance of a long-term supply of butterfly visitors*

Nectar Plants (a small sample)

Annuals

Aster	Cornflower	Cosmos
Dahlia	Globe Amaranth	Heliotrope
Lantana	Marigold	Nicotiana
Petunia	Sage	Strawflower
Sunflower	Tithonia	Zinnia

Note: *Deadheading old blossoms of annuals will increase new blooms & maximize nectar*

Perennials

Bee Balm	Butterfly weed	Chives
Coralbells	Coreopsis	Cranesbill
Echinacea	Geranium	Daisy
Daylily	Goldenrod	Joe-pye weed
Lavender	Liatris	Lythrum
Mints	Phlox	Rosemary
Rubideckia	Sedums	Violet

Note: *Fall seed pods also provide food for birds*

Shrubs — Abelia, Butterfly bush (Buddleia), privet, honeysuckle, mock-orange, spice bush

Native Plants for Butterfly Larva

Goldenrod	Milkweed	Nettle
Thistle	Tick Trefoil	Herbs
Wild grasses	Queen Anne's Lace	

Note: *Creating a hedgerow of these wild plants will make a perfect home for butterfly larva and other beneficial insects (see* **Hedgerow,** *page 57)*

Special Thought:
Your garden is a natural wildlife habitat that feeds many. A little damage to plants is natural. Most plants are hardy enough to survive losing 25% of their leaf surface to munching.

63

Gardening Resources

We hope you have been inspired to garden. Below is only a small sampling of resources, books and websites to sustain your interest and efforts. The interest in food sustainability & security is exploding! We apologize if we did not list your favorite resource. (*Note: Internet addresses may change over time*). Listed books are well-known; again with apologies for any favorites not listed. Enjoy!

LOCAL

Garden Centers
Tools, seeds, starts, plants, trees, materials, advice.
Garden Clubs
Library, bookstores, friends, neighbors, neighborhood associations

Master Gardeners, Master Composters, Master Food Preservers, Master Landscapers
Trained volunteers through the (U.S.) Cooperative Extension Service; hot-line, drop-by, educational demonstrations, advice. Locate local office: www.csrees.usda.gov/Extension

Food Bank & Community kitchens
Food sustainability
Food sharing, gleaners, nutrition-health connection, veganism, etc.

County Cooperative Extension Service
Township or Borough Council
Metro Districts
Waste Management District
Many offer free advice, consultation, brochures, select products; identify plants and insects; test soil. Drop by or call. Often have brochures & websites to support recycling, gardening and composting, etc.
Note: Your intuition, reasoning, mindfulness and resourcefulness are excellent resources, too!

ASSORTED & INTERNET

Google (search): www.google.com
Green Maven (search): www.greenmaven.com
Green People (search): www.greenpeople.org
National Wildlife Federation: www.nwf.org
American Community Gardens Association: www.communitygarden.org
National Gardening Association: www.garden.org
National Home Gardening Club: www.gardeningclub.com
Hen and Harvest Magazine (sustainable living): www.henandharvest.com
Freedom Gardens: www.freedomgardens.org
Kitchen Gardeners: www.kitchengardeners.org
Food, Not Lawns: www.foodnotlawns.com
Victory Gardens: www.revivevictorygarden.org
Kids Gardening: www.kidsgardening.org
Organic Gardening: www.organicgardening.com
Rodale (sustainable, healthy living): www.rodale.com
Mother Earth News: www.motherearthnews.com
Seeds of Change: www.seedsofchange.com
Seed Savers Exchange: www.seedsavers.org
Heirloom Seeds: www.heirloomseeds.com
Composting: www.howtocompost.org
Home Composting Made Easy: www.homecompostingmadeeasy.com
Garden Organic - UK: www.gardenorganic.org.uk
Note: Governmental agencies also have websites

Resources from Cortesia Center
84540 McBeth Rd, Eugene, Oregon, 97405 USA
1-866-837-5854 • **Email:** info@onesanctuary.com
www.onesanctuary.com • www.homecompostingmadeeasy.com
Order on the internet or call *(Prices & shipping charges subject to change)*

Home Composting Made Easy, by C. Forrest McDowell, PhD & Tricia Clark-McDowell (Cortesia Press). $4.95 (includes shipping). 32-pages, color.
The world's most popular composting guide with over 1 million copies in print!

For extensive information on home composting visit our website:
www.homecompostingmadeeasy.com
To learn about our research and products about the diverse healing qualities of the herb, Solomon's Seal visit our website: **www.solomonsseal.net**
To understand more about our work with the concept of sanctuary & peace, and to take a virtual tour of Cortesia Sanctuary visit our website: **www.onesanctuary.com**

BOOKS

GENERAL

Amazing Secrets to Growing Luscious Fruits and Vegetables at Home by Kenny Point (eZine book on internet: http://www.veggiegardeningtips.com)
Creative Vegetable Gardening by Joy Larkcom
Crockett's Victory Garden by James Crockett
Grow Your Own Vegetables by Joy Larkcom
Joy of Gardening by Dick Raymond (revered classic)
The Vegetable Gardener's Bible by Edward C. Smith
The Fast, Easy Vegetable Garden by Jerry Baker
The Garden Primer by Barbara Damrosch (classic)
The Great Vegetable Plot by Sarah Raven
The New Victory Garden by Bob Thomson (classic)
The Self-Sufficient Garden by John Seymour
The Sustainable Vegetable Garden by John Jeavons & Carol Cox (one of the best!)
Vegetable Gardening: from Planting to Picking: The Complete Guide to Creating a Bountiful Garden by Jane Courtier

Designing the New Kitchen Garden by Jennifer R. Bartley
The New Kitchen Garden by Anna Pavord
The Salad Garden by Joy Larkcom

Carrots Love Tomatoes by Louise Riotte (companion planting)
Complete Book of Companion Gardening by Bob Flowerdew

ORGANIC

Burpee: The Complete Vegetable & Herb Gardener: A Guide to Growing Your Garden Organically by Karan Davis Cutler, et al.
Four-Season Harvest: Organic Vegetables from Your Home Garden All Year Long by Eliot Coleman (any of his books are excellent!)
Organic Garden: Pocket Encyclopedia by Geoff Hamilton
Rodale's Illustrated Encyclopedia of Organic Gardening by Pauline Pears (classic)

SMALL SPACE & INTENSIVE

The All-in-One Garden: Grow Vegetables, Fruit, Herbs and Flowers in the Same Plot by Graham Rice
The Edible Container Garden by Michael Guerra
Lasagna Gardening by Patricia Lanza (vegetable gardens in small spaces)
The Postage Stamp Garden by Duane Newcomb (classic)
Square Foot Gardening by Mel Bartholomew (classic)

REFERENCE, SPECIALIZED & SUSTAINABILITY

Rodale's Vegetable Garden Problem Solver by Rodale Institute
Complete Book of Composting by Rodale Institute (classic; massive book)
Vegetables from Amaranth to Zucchini by Elizabeth Schneider
Cold Climate Gardening by Lewis Hill (geared to New England & northern U.S.)
Vegetable Gardening West of the Cascades by Steve Solomon (classic)
Gaia's Garden: A Guide to Home-Scale Permaculture by Toby Hemenway
How to Build & Use Greenhouses by T. Jeff Williams

REFERENCE, SPECIALIZED & SUSTAINABILITY (continued)

Introduction to Permaculture by Bill Mollison (classic)
Root Cellaring: Natural Cold Storage of Fruits & Vegetables by Mike Bubel
Seed to Seed: Seed Saving and Growing Tecniques for Vegetable Gardeners by Suzanne Ashworth
The Complete Book of Edible Landscaping by Rosalind Creasy (classic)
The Permaculture Home Garden by Linda Woodrow

SEED SOURCES (Internet webpages with lists of companies & organizations)

List of best seed companies (by U.S. state): http://www.motherearthnews.com/Organic-Gardening/2007-11-01/Best-Garden-Seed-Companies.aspx
Heirloom seeds sources: http://www.halcyon.com/tmend/links.htm
Seed savers, seed exchanges & seed societies: http://www.halcyon.com/tmend/exchanges.htm
"Safe Seed Pledge" seed companies *(do not knowingly buy or sell genetically engineered (GMO) seeds or plants)*: http://www.earthlypursuits.com/SeedCompanies.htm
Seed companies selling organic seed: http://www.seedalliance.org/index.php?page=Seed_Companies_Selling_Organic_Seed

---

CHILDRENS' GARDENING

Note: There are MANY books for all ages. Here's a few favorites:

A Backyard Vegetable Garden for Kids by Amie Jane Leavitt
A Beginner's Book of Vegetable Gardening by Sigmund A. Lavine
Gardening for Kids by Marylou Morano Kjelle, et. al.
I Can Grow Vegetables by David Magill
The Victory Garden Kids' Book by Marjorie Waters
Vegetables in Patches and Pots by Loreille Miller Mintz
Your First Garden Book by Marc Brown (acclaimed children's book author)

Internet Lists of Children's Gardening Books & Curriculum Materials

Children's Gardening: Books & Programmatic Materials: http://www.hort.vt.edu/HUMAN/CGbooks.html
Gardening Books for Schools & Children (this webpage was created by the University of Florida, with the assistance of the American Horticultural Society and the Cleveland Botanical Garden): http://www.gardeningsolutions.ifas.ufl.edu/schoolgardens/resources/books.shtml
Educational Programs, Curriculum Guides & Children's Gardening Activities: http://www.gardeningsolutions.ifas.ufl.edu/schoolgardens/resources/education_activities.shtml
The Herb Society of America (webpage list of children's gardening books): http://www.herbsociety.org/library/child1.php

---

GARDEN AS SANCTUARY (selected titles)

The Sanctuary Garden: Creating a Place of Refuge in Your Yard and Garden by Christopher Forrest McDowell & Tricia Clark-McDowell (classic)
Cultivating Sacred Space: Gardening for the Soul by Elizabeth Murray
Sanctuary: Gardening for the Soul by Dency Kane
Spiritual Gardening: Creating Sacred Space Outdoors by Peg Streep
The Garden Sanctuary: Creating Outdoor Space to Soothe the Soul by Keith Mitchell
The Healing Garden: Gardening for the Mind, Body and Soul by Gay Search